MW00876073

POLICY vs. PAPER CLIPS

*how using the corporate model makes a
nonprofit board more efficient & effective*

EUGENE H. FRAM WITH VICKI BROWN

3rd Edition
updated and expanded

Library of Congress Cataloging-in Publication Data

Fram, Eugene H.
Policy vs. Paper Clips: How Using the Corporate Model Makes a Nonprofit Board More Efficient & Effective/ Eugene H. Fram with Vicki Brown.—Updated and expanded 3rd ed.

ISBN: 1456374052
ISBN 13: 9781456374051
LCCN: 2010917668

1. Nonprofit organizations—management - governance I. Brown, Vicki
II. Title
HD62.6.F73 2011

Volume 3489, Page 881, United States Copyright Office
eugenefram@yahoo.com

Policy vs. Paper Clips *shows how to transform your organization by optimizing:*

Strategic Planning
- Focus an organization on strategic issues over operational minutiae
- Encourage directors to bring their own special expertise and cultural values to board decisions

Board Structure
- Develop or enhance a mission focused board structure for growth
- Use ad hoc committees more effectively to obtain more timely results
- Designate the senior manager as the president/CEO to give position more prestige
- Establish a framework for separating policy development from operational activities
- Make effective use of an executive committee
- Reduce or increase board size
- Make wise use of volunteers' time to make board recruitment easier
- Operate effectively with only three standing board committees
- Make major board structural changes with minimal disruption

- Develop effective audit committee procedures
- Keep board involvement high when developing policies and strategies

Board-Staff Relations

- Create a partnership between board and staff built on trust
- Pinpoint management's responsibility and clarify its accountability
- Allow for more management flexibility to develop a more entrepreneurial culture
- Increase focus on productivity at the expense of bureaucratic processes
- Develop a more professional and self-managing staff
- Build board respect for the management team
- Evaluate the senior manager fairly despite only having imperfect metrics
- Build a working relationship between the volunteer chair and the CEO
- Improve the CEO's fund-raising capacity to drive development productivity

Operations and Compliance

- Sharpen the organization's client focus to improve mission impact
- Obtain greater efficiencies through lower costs

- Establish a system of organizational checks and balances
- Use the board to provide responsibility for – and oversight over — fraud prevention
- Understand the implications of the Sarbanes-Oxley Act and the Intermediate Sanctions Act
- Understand the need for – and implement – rigorous assessment of operational outcomes

CONTENTS

THE AUTHOR'S MAILBOX
Reprinted from the Second Edition

R ecently a thank-you letter arrived in my office. A thank-you letter is always nice, but this one was special. It underscored in very tangible ways what a significant difference the Corporate Model can make for a nonprofit organization, even when the nonprofit is very successful.

The letter was written by Mary Glick, then president and CEO of a Delaware not-for-profit group with an annual operating budget of $1 million, a paid staff of fourteen, and hundreds of volunteers.

Though this nonprofit distributes more than three million pounds of food annually to needy people, her letter wasn't about the group's work, but about how the nonprofit worked. She described developments that had occurred in the years since she had been hired as the first paid executive of a seven-year-old food bank. A portion of her letter follows.

Dear Dr. Fram,

... For the first several years, the board and I worked on the difficult task of moving from board management to staff management of operations.

After four years, times seemed good, on the surface. We appeared to have made the adjustment.

Programs were growing, and we had just completed our first capital campaign, purchased land, and built a warehouse.

Board members were enthusiastic.

On the other hand, I was becoming concerned that, more and more, the issues I thought were "policy implementation" the board felt were "policy making" and vice versa.

Even though we didn't have any significant misunderstandings, board meetings became very stressful because I felt that it was only a matter of time before a major problem would arise.

Performance reviews were even more stressful because the criteria for success kept changing. Sometimes the criteria measured something tangible but not necessarily pertinent.

Fortunately, there was a high level of trust and respect between board members and myself. Top officers were willing to take my concerns seriously and were open and supportive of my search for solutions. Luckily, during that search I received a copy of your book, Policy vs. Paper Clips.

The most important aspect of your model for our board was your suggested organizational structure. We had already spent some time discussing board governance responsibilities. We had agreed that strategic planning and assessment, using meaningful, predetermined measures, were key. But until we read your book (and it is now a standard part of our board's annual orientation), we couldn't picture what kind of structure would adequately support those objectives.

Dr. Fram, your model simplified my life tremendously. Since we adopted it, I'm no longer expected to "read board members' minds" on important issues. We agree in advance on our goals, measures, and expectations. We then prioritize them and put them in writing. It is now clear to everyone involved that my job is to accomplish those goals, making the best use of volunteer and staff resources. Now our board meetings are to the point, productive, and generally last one to one and one-half hours.

With the growing number of nonprofits adopting your model, you may have new information you can share. I want you to know that if you plan to update your book, I'll be among the first to read it.

Best of luck and thank you.

MARY E. GLICK
President and CEO
Food Bank of Delaware

RECENT E-MAILS

From Chicago, Illinois

Our nonprofit human services organization celebrated our sixtieth anniversary in 2010. In 2007, we began to transform the governance structure of our organization based upon the principles described in Policy vs. Paper Clips by Dr. Eugene Fram.

It took us about nine months to research the issues and decide to make the changes. We have now operated under the new structure since July 2008. The new structure follows closely with the one that is described in Dr. Fram's book. We have three board committees (Executive, Assessment, and Planning and Resources).

As with any transition, there are challenges, pitfalls, and moments of enlightenment. We had no board turnover attributed to the changes. The consensus from our board is that we now have much more beneficial discussion at board meetings and board members feel they have more say in the strategy and direction of the organization.

If anyone is interested in learning more about our organization's experience feel free to contact me (Dan Strick) at dstrick@southstarservices. org.

From Palo Alto, California

I had Policy vs. Paper Clips on the bleachers beside me when I was sitting at my son's early morning soccer game yesterday. A dad next to me picked it up, flipped through it, asked about it, and said his wife is on a number of boards and would be interested in it. He pulled out his hand-held and bought it, right there on the spot.

Author's Note:

My response to nonprofit leaders who want to know more about the Corporate Model is contained in this updated third edition of *Policy vs. Paper Clips.*

FOREWARD

Peter Goldberg

Since publication of the 1995 edition of *Policy vs. Paper Clips*, a lot has happened to motivate nonprofit organizations in the United States to take a close look at how they govern themselves.

Most notably the passage of Sarbanes-Oxley in 2002 and the focus on governance and transparency conveyed in the new 990s reframe public expectations of how nonprofit boards function. Rather than resisting change, high-performing nonprofits are embracing the message and seizing new opportunities to strengthen the governance function.

An equally compelling motivation for self-examination has been the increasingly complex and challenging environment in which nonprofits operate. At a time when the world struggles with economic challenges, it takes enormous time and energy to lead a nonprofit organization and ensure that it is prepared to meet tomorrow's demand for services. For those who volunteer at nonprofits, it is also more important than ever that their volunteer time be as productive as possible. Ours is a world in which people live time-compressed lives, and time for volunteer commitments is a precious commodity.

No organization can afford to squander the hours its volunteer directors donate. At the same time, volunteer directors and executives should not be so busy "giving their time" that they fail to assess how well they conduct business.

That's why this book is valuable for every nonprofit organization that wants to know where it is and where it's going. Reading this book will prompt many people involved in the nonprofit sector to reexamine and redefine the roles of their board of directors, chief executive, and staff. Whether or not your organization ultimately adopts the Corporate Model, it will gain from such scrutiny. The result of taking time for a thorough self-examination will be an organization that does its job better.

My personal experience with the Corporate Model in a nonprofit environment spans fifteen years as a president and CEO of a national nonprofit organization and as an international consultant. I have seen how effectively and efficiently it facilitates strategic planning by building a partnership between board and staff. In essence, it provides management with the opportunity to focus on continuing concerns and enables policymakers to focus on the future.

Over the years, member agencies have come to appreciate many of the other strengths of the Model. Cost effectiveness ranks high. The Model also promotes professional growth among staff by encouraging staff members to rely on their own expertise rather than a lengthy committee process to solve problems. Staff members are what they should be—professionals who provide information and make recommendations to the board. Moreover, the board determines its strategy based on consideration of the important issues rather than fragmented committee concerns. Volunteer directors and executives accomplish more, in less time.

Much of the interest in the Corporate Model within my own organization is due to Eugene Fram, who has conducted numerous seminars and workshops for our member agencies and for countless other nonprofit groups. His experience with the Model dates to 1975. Consequently, he has built on thirty-five years of experience in developing this third edition, based on varied tenures as board director, board chair, author and consultant. Not so long ago I checked out Amazon and found the 1995 edition being sold for as much as $100 for a used copy! My advice is to reach for this third edition because it provides additional new information while retaining crucial information from the first two editions.

When you read this book, you'll find it is useful for anyone interested in promoting effectiveness, efficiency, and strategic planning as integral components in the management of a nonprofit organization. For organizations currently using the Model, it serves as a guidebook for continuing evaluation. Ultimately, those who will benefit most are the people you work so hard to serve.

Peter Goldberg is President & CEO,
Alliance for Children & Families,
Milwaukee, Wisconsin

PREFACE

Based on available information, it is estimated that about 1.5 million nonprofit organizations currently operate in the United States. (Their numbers are likely growing because nationally the IRS reports it receives, on the average day, about 180 new applications for tax-exempt status, including applications for secular not-for-profit, religious, and other groups.) Measuring nonprofits' impact on society is probably impossible, although I suspect that their impact is much bigger than most Americans realize.

Consider that, in New York City alone, estimates indicate that $4 billion, or about 10 percent of the city's budget, is spent on contracted services, under which nonprofit groups provide such services as health care, job training, and youth programs. This is roughly double the percentage of the budget allocated in the mid-1990s. Although most people think of the Big Apple as a center for financial services and the apparel trade, they would probably be surprised to learn that New York City's nonprofit groups employ hundreds of thousands more people than either of these industries.

Without a doubt, nonprofit organizations—including human service agencies, trade associations, educational institutions, and professional associations—play a vital role in this country.

While few of our largest manufacturing organizations exist one hundred years after their founding, many of the country's significant nonprofits do. The Alliance for Children & Families is just one of many such organizations that are either approaching or have already reached the one-hundred-year anniversary mark. Yet nonprofit agencies could do their jobs even better. They could, that is, if they were better managed and governed.

As management consultant Peter Drucker has pointed out, with the exception of a small group of nonprofits led by trailblazing leaders, management standards at nonprofits are often low. While some of the best nonprofit managers have completed self-improvement programs offered by universities and professional groups, it seems volunteer directors, who rotate through board positions, often want to cling to traditional governance formats. Typically, that means centering board attention on day-to-day operational issues instead of tapping the board's creative energies to focus on critical issues involving vision, direction, and adapting to new challenges and capturing emerging opportunities.

David Simms, a partner in The Bridgespan Group, a nonprofit consulting group, commented in a recent *Harvard Business Review* blog that few nonprofit directors' meeting agendas reflect strategic issues such as how to increase staff or board diversity and offer services with greater impact. As a result, nonprofit boards are not succeeding in their roles to focus on strategic issues.

Results of a 2010 Board Source survey of approximately 1,000 chief executives and 800 board members and chairs underscore the same point.

Among the key survey results are these: chief executives give their boards an overall grade of C+ and 45 percent of boards receive a "C or below" grade for strategic planning.[1]

The need to raise standards has never been greater. Harsh realities currently affect the environment in which nonprofit groups operate. Budgets are tight. Funding cutbacks are not only common but also increasingly painful as the United States endures challenging economic and politically turbulent times. Along with substantial financial constraints, nonprofit organizations face increased demand for their services. In other words, resources are tighter and client and member needs are growing. These are very difficult times for nonprofits.

New management environments and directions, such as the use of social media and new information technologies, affect all groups. Many institutions, including business, political, social, governmental, and academic bodies, have had to adjust to changing conditions.

Nonprofits cannot continue to operate as they have in the past. For most, it is no longer possible for a group of volunteer directors to be involved in the day-to-day operations of the organization. In fact, volunteer directors who micromanage their

---

1 "*Board Source Nonprofit Governance Index 2010*, November 2010.

agencies are, in blunt terms, cost centers for non-profits, since they affect staff time so dramatically. At the same time, the valued executive director of the past, who worked his or her way up through the ranks, now needs more than direct-service experience in the field to lead a twenty-first-century nonprofit organization. He or she needs administrative ability and a strong desire to manage an organization. She or he must be a leader, an innovator, and a communicator, all at once. Today's nonprofit executive directors also need creative, effective boards.

Thus, the role of the volunteer board of directors must change. The need for governance change does not negate the successes achieved by volunteer boards in the past; it is merely a reflection of the fact that growth brings new responsibilities. Since volunteer responsibilities may conflict with greater demands to meet family and work commitments, recruiting qualified volunteer directors has become more difficult.

But bottom line, good governance simply makes fiscal sense. Good governance helps eliminate the many hidden costs associated with pursuing activities that have nothing to do with the organization's purpose. For example, board directors who pursue projects that are worthwhile but unrelated to the organization's mission contribute to their organization's hidden costs. So does the staff human resource director who must spend an inordinate amount of time providing routine operating information to board members.

Board agendas must be cleared of operational issues, issues that paid professional staff can best resolve. Board discussions should center on policy issues—vision, mission, values, and evaluation of programs and goals.

By eliminating operating issues from agendas, the board has time to move into what Harvard's Bill Ryan refers to as the generative mode. According to Ryan, boards in a generative mode can come to grips with "what if" and other long-term questions. Because directors' questions in this mode are different from the questions that they ask when day-to-day operations take up the agenda, they will find themselves focused on identifying available opportunities and vulnerabilities. This enables board members to tap their special expertise and professional experience in board discussions. To draw upon this outside wealth of knowledge and perspectives, nonprofit executives should avoid acculturating board members to the "conventional wisdom" of the organization. (In practical terms that means, for example, that a director with marketing strategy experience should be asked to help uncover new markets to serve but not asked to write advertising copy.) Following are several examples of generative questions:

Identifying an opportunity
- Museum boards asking: "What are the long-term impacts of selling long-unshown antiques to private dealers?"

- Children's residential organizations asking: "To what extent might we also provide living facilities for the elderly?"

Identifying a vulnerability
- Counseling agency boards considering: "What is the impact of more sophisticated use of new drug therapies on the need for counseling therapy?"
- Symphony orchestras asking: "As our core audiences age, how can we interest younger audiences in classical music?"

Separating operational and policy issues is more complicated than it sounds. It requires a fundamental change in a nonprofit's culture and promotes new relationships and communication styles from the top to the bottom rung of the organization.

This book proposes to strengthen nonprofit boards and to improve their productivity through an organizational format called the Corporate Model. Although the switch to the Corporate Model is not easy to achieve, it is, I assure you, worth the effort.

I've been watching the growth of the Corporate Model since 1975, when I conducted a field experiment to implement it the first time. It was immediately copied by others; those who have adopted the Model report that it works. Based on long experience, I personally believe it is most effective for nonprofit organizations that have annual budgets of at about $1 million and staffs of at about fifteen.

Based on the sales of the first two editions of the book and the robust aftermarket that has developed for used copies, I now estimate that thousands of nonprofits have tried and adopted the Model. Recently a nonprofit president/CEO with 2,200-employees wrote me, "While I was not at [this organization at the time the Corporate Model was adopted], I count your presentation to our board (members) and their subsequent actions as a key period in our governance history."

Though mature at age thirty-five, the Corporate Model for nonprofit boards is still considered controversial in some nonprofit sectors. It flies against a tradition of involving volunteers in staff and management operations. It has to be tailored to the needs of individual organizations. Why? Because one-size-fits-all governance models simply do not work in the nonprofit world.

This is a serious book about a serious subject, but it is far from dull reading. It is written in a lively and interesting way to capture the attention and imagination of both volunteer directors and nonprofit managers. Read it and you will no longer have to whisper about how your organization needs to change the way it operates.

You will know how to push for change. In the process of making the change, you will help make your nonprofit a more dynamic organization.

EUGENE H. FRAM
Los Altos, California

INTRODUCTION

*W*hen this book was in the conceptual stage, I found myself faced with two choices—take a nuts-and-bolts ("boring") approach to explaining the Corporate Model or find a way to make the Model come alive by telling a story that would connect with real people, and inspire them to make meaningful change in their own organizations. That's why this book, with the assistance of the highly talented Vicki Brown, is built around an exchange of e-mails between two old friends who have ties to very different nonprofit organizations.

Russ was recently appointed to serve on a nonprofit board that has the traditional community model. He is extremely frustrated by the board's involvement in operational issues and the plodding way in which decisions are reached. He vents his frustrations to his friend Jack.

Jack's board and line administrative experience in nonprofit groups is extensive. He is now the president and CEO of a nonprofit organization that has operated under the Corporate Model for approximately four years.

Although Russ and Jack are fictional characters, the material contained in their letters and other communications is drawn from numerous case studies, records, speeches, interviews, blogs, my volunteer experiences and my professional consulting observations of nonprofit groups. The book draws most heavily upon my experience as a volunteer director. Every situation or example was developed from a real nonprofit world experience. Only names and nonprofit settings were changed.

Taken as a whole, the e-mails and other information illustrate how a nonprofit organization can adopt—in a practical, not a theoretical way—the Corporate Model format for its own board. Jack and Russ provide rational solutions to the current problems faced by nonprofit organizations—problems that nonprofit director and chief executives will instantly recognize.

ACKNOWLEDGMENTS

I have encountered many outstanding chief executives and volunteer board members in the past 35 years in a wide variety of nonprofit organizations. Their successes and challenges are captured on the pages of this book. Without them this book would never have been written. I'm grateful for all they taught me.

1

THE CORPORATE MODEL

A Board Alternative

From: Russ Peterson
Sent: September 15 10:20 PM
To: Jack Billings
Subject: What a waste of time!

Jack,

Today I wasted ANOTHER two hours on the Yorkville board of directors. I can't begin to tell you how frustrated I am. We just give too much time to minor items such as vehicle repair bills, office dividers, and refuse contracts. The important things never seem to be discussed.

I don't have much experience with nonprofit boards, but after only one year on this one I'm ready to quit. That's sad. I thought I'd be involved in significant discussions and help chart the organization's future. How incredibly naive!

Seems to me a lot of the other directors like the way the board operates. The place could be bankrupt and no one would notice.

As an old friend and veteran executive director, please give me your reaction. Is there another alternative? Or should I resign now?

Russ

BTW: want to be clear where I'm coming from. I'm not sorry you recommended me for this board. I'm just sorry the board isn't more effective.

From: Jack Billings
Sent: September 16 8:43 PM
To: Russ Peterson
Subject: What a waste of time!

Hey, Russ –

Your e-mail struck some nerves! Your frustration is understandable. But DON'T RESIGN!
And don't be deterred from making your feelings
known just because you've been on the board for
only a year. You probably have some board colleagues who feel the way you do. If you're this
frustrated, others must be too. I suspect they'd
make comments that echo your own.

I can relate to what's happening on your board. I
grew up professionally with the system you describe. Agendas that seem endless, committee
meetings that last hours, heated exchanges about
personnel decisions, lengthy discussions about
$100 items—but never enough time to discuss
long-range needs or ways to meet them.

I'll wager that in the year you've been on the
Yorkville board, you've been approached by
disgruntled staff members; dealt with countless
questions about individual salaries, evaluations,
and promotions; and heard committee report
after committee report. Very likely your board

always has plans to talk about directions, priorities, and goals but never quite gets to them.

Boards like yours have been around for years. My own agency's board was structured just like it when I came here as executive director six years ago. But no longer.

We've been operating under a new board and management structure for four years now. It's called the Corporate Model. The Model takes its name from the business world because, like well-structured corporate boards, it clearly separates operational issues from policy.

Everyone I know who has tried the Model agrees it works. The Model makes nonprofits more professional, more flexible, and more efficient. Most important, we're able to focus more on the client groups we serve. Making the switch is well worth the result. However, it is certainly a major shift and the changeover does not occur without problems.

Why? Because the Model requires a fundamental change in behavior. Directors must be willing to give up the operating power they have in traditionally structured not-for-profit groups. The top executive must be comfortable making decisions and taking risks. We're in a new era and must operate in a different kind of environment. Nonprofits are under tremendous pressure from donors, government, clients, and others who provide funds or receive services.

The Corporate Model can be adopted by nonprofit groups that have grown beyond the point where a volunteer board can oversee day-to-day activities. It's an excellent alternative for your Yorkville board.

Send me an e-mail if you want more details. I don't want to tell you more about the Corporate Model than you might want to know.

BTW: Regarding my comment above about well-structured business boards.
I do stay abreast of business news and certainly am aware that ALL business boards are not well structured!

Hang in there…

Jack

From: Russ Peterson
Sent: October 7 7:10 AM
To: Jack Billings
Subject: Not sure I'm ready

Jack,

I've read and reread your last e-mail a number of times and I've decided to give the job another year. But I'm not sure I'm ready to push for a whole new approach on our board—though, I must admit, your Corporate Model sounds interesting.

Have had time to reassess since firing off that e-mail after a particularly frustrating board session. I keep telling myself that I need to readjust some people's thinking, not revise the Yorkville board's structure. After all, the board has had the same structure for many years, and the organization has done a reasonably credible job. Most of the staff are quite dedicated. Many remind me of you when you were working directly with clients.

It's definitely time for some changes. I'm staying on next year in the hope I can be a part of these changes. I think I can do it without a whole new approach.

I value your comments. Thanks for the support!

Russ

From: Russ Peterson
Sent: October 14 9:12 PM
To: Jack Billings
Subject: Tedious debate—again!

Jack,

Delete my last e-mail! I'm angry again and now admit my frustration runs deep. Bottom line: the Yorkville board is ineffective!

Why the turnaround? Let me tell you about yesterday's board "meeting." We scheduled it for the evening so that everyone would be able to stay to talk about important issues. In fact, there were just three items on the agenda: executive director remarks, discussion of long-range financial needs, and ways to raise funds. With rising costs and a growing elderly population, we face some major financial hurdles. What we decide now is going to have an impact on the organization for years to come.

The executive director's report on operations was supposed to last only twenty minutes. Instead, his comments sparked a tedious debate that lasted two and a half hours! Happens every time any minor adjustment of fees comes up. Then we ended up discussing whether the top exec should

be authorized to buy a minivan or an SUV to re-
place an aging vehicle.

By 10:45 p.m. everyone was exhausted. Long-
range planning was tabled AGAIN. When Bob,
a board veteran, made a parting comment, it was
suddenly crystal clear to me that Yorkville can't
afford to operate according to the status quo.
Some big problems are emerging, but the board
isn't on top of them.

"Too bad about tabling the planning agenda,"
Bob said, "but I think it was a healthy airing of
everyone's feelings about our fees." I didn't say
what I was thinking. "Feelings are fine, but we
didn't accomplish anything."

We made some minor adjustments in the fee
structure. None of us knows how these adjustments will affect the organization's budget. It's
a critical issue. We may have to make some staff
reductions if certain funding trends continue.
Does this happen with your board?

And, oh, about that minivan vs. SUV debate.
We agreed with the ED's recommendation—we
should buy a minivan. Does such a minor decision really require twenty-five people and forty-
five minutes of discussion on your board? That's
nineteen person hours!

Help! Tell me more about the Corporate Model!

Russ

FYI: The family is looking forward to our get-together at Thanksgiving. I know Paul, who's a senior now, wants to ask your college freshman what it's REALLY like out there.

From: Jack Billings
Sent: October 26 8:02 AM.
To: Russ Peterson
Subject: The Model—one step at a time

Russ –

Four years ago my board of directors switched my title from "executive director" to "president and CEO." The switch created a wave of positive and negative comments, both in the agency and in agencies with which we partner. Some applauded the move, saying it was about time that nonprofit managers get recognized for the management contributions they make, but others grumbled that organizations like ours were becoming too "businesslike." One staff member even cautioned us not to lose our "social work virginity to a business philosophy."

But my new title was the beginning of sweeping changes that would affect everyone in the organization to some extent. (Here's just one example: all my direct reports were given vice president titles—formerly they were called directors.) I'm glad to say that my job and those of my management staff haven't been the same since. The new title was a major step in communicating to the staff and public who was responsible for agency operations. The Model made it all possible.

But I don't want to inundate you with endless details about the Model. I think you'll really see its value if I can show you how it comes alive. The best approach, I think, is to send you a series of e-mails. Send your feedback, questions, reactions and we'll take this one step at a time if you want to hear more about the Model.

First, though, let me tell you why my nonprofit adopted the Corporate Model. When I joined this organization six years ago, I was ready to manage. Board members assured me they didn't want to be involved in operational decision making. I was hired, they said, because of both my managerial and my direct-service expertise.

But problems surfaced rather quickly. The culprit—the cause of my problems—was tradition. Some board members were used to discussing individual salaries, being involved with promotion decisions, and working directly with clients without staff involvement! In addition, there was deep mistrust of terminology or officer titles used in the for-profit sector (or even by some large nonprofit foundations!).

At that time, some of my board members were convinced we could become the human service equivalent of a baby-sized Enron. A lot of this had to do with the fact that my agency was the first in the community to make the change. At the time, even the operating head of the local United Way had "executive vice president" as his title, and a volunteer board member carried the title "president/CEO."

I now know that the volunteers who held the title, each for a year, finally were informed by a then new member of their board (a lawyer!) that the CEO designation also exposed each one of them to increased personal liability, which properly should rest with the full-time person responsible for operations. Why the hesitancy in giving a CEO title to the operating manager? My own agency's attorney, who is an experienced nonprofit director, once commented, "Unfortunately, this occurs because many believe that the term 'CEO' may trigger perceptions of corporate greed and profit motivation instead of charity and public benefit."

Because of tradition and mistrust, managerial responsibility in my organization was compromised. The board was seen as the final authority in many operational matters related to human resources and finances. This is likely the situation today on your Yorkville board, and frankly you have lots of company in nonprofit organizations across the U.S.

Even in an area as vital as the development of our budget, it was difficult to pinpoint where my responsibility and the board's began and ended. It was a system of so-called "shared responsibility," which could lead to "shared blame" when something went wrong. (Side story to help make this point: one small human service agency in this community did a great job for its clients for decades, using funding that came mainly from government sources. When several key state grant pools disappeared, the agency folded. Neither the board nor the exec recognized the strategic problem that was before them since their meetings focused on operational details. The client group being served was devastated. Quietly, the directors blamed the exec for a lack of leadership, and the exec viewed his job as doing what his board directed him to accomplish.)

Roll back time to when I first came to my agency. Because the decision-making line between management, my board, and the board's complex committee structure had never been clear (on paper, the organizational chart looked like a spaghetti factory with lines going everywhere), communications were often confusing. It was commonplace for a staff member to make an "end run" to a board member whenever he or she did not like a management decision. In one instance, I passed over a staff person for a promotion, and he called one of the most influential board members to complain. The board member (a tax expert with no managerial· experience) told the staff person and then me that I had made a mistake. I diplomatically blew my stack on that one! Nonprofit senior managers have to remind themselves constantly that although many of their directors may have significant positions in business and professional organizations, that does not necessarily mean they have had extensive managerial experience.

Given the advantage of hindsight, I now admit that I did not properly assess how heavy a burden tradition can be. I became increasingly discouraged and wondered whether I had made a mistake in relocating and accepting the job. There was a lot of soul searching, but it was clear to me that my family wasn't interested in relocating again.

Russ, I need to stop. It's now 8:30 a.m., voice mail is blinking, e-mails are piling up, and my administrative aide has a list of my appointments and tells me a donor just came in unannounced! To be continued…

Jack

From: Jack Billings
Sent: November 1 6:45 PM
To: Russ Peterson
Subject: Why we decided to change

Russ –

Just reviewed my last e-mail to you. I had taken
you up to the point where I was considering quit-
ting my job. I'm glad I didn't. Instead I took my
deep concerns to the board.

I told my board of directors I found our meetings exhausting. Our agendas were loaded with
operational items, and policy issues were often
postponed or even ignored. Sometimes meeting quorums were difficult to convene because
some of the more knowledgeable board members were bored with the minutiae and our slow
decision-making process. Because of the way
we operated, we had countless committee meetings, overlapping concerns, and repeated questions. In turn, these drained staff time and the
organization's resources. Our style meant board
members were needlessly involved in operational matters, even though some directors thoroughly enjoyed being involved. As a result, my
management responsibilities were made more
difficult. Worst of all, I told them, I did not think

we were planning properly for the organization's future.

I was somewhat surprised to learn that about half
the board shared, to some extent, my concerns
about our board operation and structure. The
other half felt that everything had worked for
years, so why change? That first frank discussion
led to the formation of a board study committee. Fortunately, it was chaired by a person with
board experience in both the profit and nonprofit
sectors. She really understood the need to separate operational decisions from policy issues.

Our search led us to the Corporate Model. The
concept behind the Model is simply stated. The
board sets policy. The top professional manager
oversees operations. Eventually, this concept becomes a part of the organization's culture.

The Corporate Model appeals to me because I
believe a nonprofit's efficiency and effectiveness have become critically important. My four
reasons:

Public funding cuts (and fund-raising challenges) are here to stay. Our clients have more needs
than our supporters can afford, so we must focus,
more than ever, on results.

Long-term planning is key to improving results.

Board members must set the tone for long-range planning. They need to have time to do that job well. When you consider the time-compressed schedules most board people have today, it's essential to conserve their time for the truly important issues.

Foundations, donors, and governmental agencies are demanding we become more transparent about how effectively and efficiently we serve our clients.

BTW: Forgot to mention earlier that the person on your board who appreciated "the healthy airing of everyone's feelings about fees" is probably a process person. Be aware of this type of personality. It's very common to find them on nonprofit boards. More about overemphasizing process and the proponents of process later.

Russ, this e-mail is already getting too long, but before I shut down my computer, I want to quickly relate a couple of stories from situations I've observed.

Harry Crown, Executive Director

Crown was a frustrated executive director of a national trade association. He had single-handedly built the organization, while being heavily micromanaged by his board and hampered by the board's process of electing a new president each year. However, despite these management limitations, he was able to develop a $5 million fund reserve over his fifteen-year tenure by offering seminars, publishing a magazine, and having well-attended annual meetings.

The level of board control he experienced is not unusual when executive director positions are employed, as they are required in organizations' embryo stages. Board members of start-up nonprofits feel a need to tell the executive director "exactly what to do." But the process continues, even when the organization flourishes.

After fifteen years, Crown could make a maximum expenditure of only $5,000 without board approval. (One simple switch in telephone communications cost $6,000!) He resigned and purchased an apple farm in order to use his creative talents better.

John Smith, President/CEO

Smith, at age forty-five, decided to leave an industry position to head a national association
representing more than 275 local groups. He was
named president/CEO and given substantial operational decision autonomy. Only strategic issues
are referred to his three board committees and
then presented to the full board. Now some fifteen
years later, he heads an organization with well
over four hundred local groups. There have been
bumps in the road to achieve this level of success,
but he is considered one of the nation's outstanding nonprofit leaders. He knows the autonomy,
trust, and rigorous outcome evaluations that go
along with the president/CEO title have supported
his efforts to keep his organization growing.

Clearly Crown wasn't operating under the
Corporate Model, but Smith is. But remember,
Russ, the Corporate Model is not a quick fix.
Change is difficult.

Do you think the Corporate Model still sounds
appropriate for Yorkville? I think I can provide
the most important information. If you are interested in taking a leading role at Yorkville, I'm
happy to help.

Jack

BTW: Just remembered you asked me two questions I should answer. Under the Corporate Model, the board never worries about buying a minivan versus an SUV. Such decisions are the responsibility of the top manager. Also, under the Model, the board approves the budget and management sets the sliding fee scale to responsibly meet budgeted income requirements. It's easy to see why this occurs if you think about the concept behind the Corporate Model:

THE BOARD SETS POLICY. THE TOP MANAGER IS RESPONSIBLE FOR OPERATIONS.

It's already 1:30 so we'll postpone the rest of the agenda till next meeting.

2

THE CORPORATE MODEL

Professionalism Flexibility

Efficiency

From: Russ Peterson
Sent: November 11 7:30 AM
To: Jack Billings
Subject: What do we do first?

Jack,

I've forwarded your e-mails to several of my fellow Yorkville board members. Got some interesting reactions. The most consistent reaction was "Let's investigate." Seems I'm NOT the only one who's frustrated with the way the board operates. All three people with whom I talked want to consider a new course.

So, what do we do first?

Russ

From: Jack Billings
Sent: November 13 7:45 AM
To: Russ Peterson
Subject: Start this way

Russ –

The first step in investigating change is to get a board committee appointed to look at where your board is right now. The committee should review the present board structure, determine the need for change, and list options for the future.

Part of the work will involve a priority listing of current board problems. You've hinted that Yorkville may have to face staffing cutbacks. Other issues that jump out at me as I quickly review our e-mail exchanges:

- rising costs to serve an aging population
- board members' frustration over lack of time for planning, which may be jeopardizing the organization's future
- problems in communication among staff, management, and board

Before your board can go anywhere, it has to be convinced that the present system needs modification. If your board is typical, it will be divided into several groups on this issue: 1) people who want change, 2) people opposed to change (some staunchly so), and 3) what I call process people.

Process people like to sit back and look at things. They always ask, "Have we consulted everybody?" or say, "Let's make sure we have considered everything." Often they are the people who call for a postponement of the vote, even after a lengthy discussion.

Process people are well-intentioned, sincere individuals. However, you have to be careful that these people don't continue to look at one angle after another until they lose sight of the committee's main job. They can keep action in limbo indefinitely!

The good news is you have colleagues on the Yorkville board who are ready to take action. In my experience, boards often lose some of their best volunteers, who get frustrated and quietly resign. Their usual reason for resigning is "the pressure of current job obligations." To me, that's a covert message that the board is getting mired in minutiae. I have a good friend, an excellent volunteer director on a couple of boards here in town, who recently used "heavy job obligations" as his reason for resigning from a board. The real reason, he confided to me, was the executive director used board meeting time inappropriately, including asking the full board to review detailed public relations PowerPoint presentations.

The first and third groups (people who want change and process people) will be very willing to appoint a committee. Process people, in fact, like to look at options.

But remember, you want a working committee, one that's not too large. You're not looking for a one-hundred-page report. I hope you, Russ, will be a member of this committee. The Corporate Model should be an option for committee members to examine.

I'll give you chapter and verse on how the Model works, starting next week when you come for Thanksgiving.

Jack

From: Jack Billings
Sent: November 13 7:59 AM.
To: Russ Peterson
Subject: Meant to send this!
Attachment: Statement adopted by board.pdf

Russ –

Meant to e-mail this as well—but here it is now!

Attached find the formal statement of board responsibilities developed by my board when we adopted the Corporate Model. After you read it, I'm sure you will have questions we can discuss in person. If your board opts for the Corporate Model, one of the first things it will need is a board statement. It's the initial tool needed to achieve the separation of policy and operations required by the Model.

And note the date at the bottom of the attached— just goes to show that some things stay "evergreen." Just reread the document and realized it still works!

BOARD OF DIRECTORS' FUNCTIONS*

The board of directors establishes and monitors corporate policy. The board operates through the president/ chief executive officer (CEO). The CEO, in turn, executes policy and is responsible for the prudent and creative operations of the organization. In this role, the CEO exercises leadership resulting in the effective and efficient use of board and non-board members' time. The board:

A. Directs management
1. Establishes long-term organizational objectives
2. Sets overall policy affecting strategies designed to achieve objectives
3. Employs the CEO

B. Judges management action
1. Evaluates short-term and long-term performance of management
2. Determines whether policies are being carried out and goals achieved

C. Approves management action
1. Critically reviews, approves, or disapproves proposals in policy areas (for example, major capital needs or expenditures and major contracts)

2. Provides formal recognition and acceptance of executive decisions when related to operational concerns

D. Advises management
Acts in an advisory or consultative capacity on operations when sought by management

E. Receives information from management
Regularly receives reports on the organization (e.g., performance, program development, external factors, concerns)

F. Acts as a public and community relations resource to management
Keeps the organization attuned to the external environment in which it operates

*Adapted from John A. Grobey, "Making the Board of Directors More Effective,"
California Management Review 16 (Spring 1974): 25-34.

From: Russ Peterson
Sent: November 22 9:50 PM
To: Jack Billings
Subject: Heads up!

Jack—heads up on the questions I'll have for you
when we talk over the holiday!

1. *How does the Corporate Model make a
    nonprofit more professional?*
2. *More flexible?*
3. *More efficient?*
4. *What are its limitations?*
5. *If the top executive has all the operational
    control, what kind of assessment is he or she
    subject to?*
6. *Who sets salaries—for example, of a top
    VP?*
7. *How do you avoid "end runs" (such as the
    staff nurse who came to me last week com-
    plaining she was being treated unfairly)?*
8. *What is the importance of the title change,
    say, from executive director to president and
    CEO?*
9. *Looks to me like the Model calls for a tre-
    mendous amount of trust between CEO and
    board. Aren't you creating a whole new en-
    vironment here?*
10. *Isn't this kind of formal and businesslike for
    a nonprofit organization?*

Russ

From: Russ Peterson
Sent: December 15 7:22 PM
To: Jack Billings
Subject: Did I capture the key points?
Attachment: Notes on the Model

Jack,

It always seems to take awhile to settle in after a wonderful vacation. Thanks to you and Ann for all the good company and wonderful food. As always, our kids thoroughly enjoyed being with your two teenagers.

My primary reason for sending this e-mail, however, is to thank you for the time spent talking about the inner workings of the Corporate Model. I also want to be certain that I too understand it, before I ask the board to appoint a committee to evaluate our current structure.

Look at the notes I've attached. Are there any other key points that you think I should add?

Look forward to your feedback!

Russ

NOTES ON THE CORPORATE MODEL

1. The issue of increased board professionalism. The quality of board activity improves as discussions take on a policy flavor. Important decisions can be more fully developed in meetings. The talents of board members can be used more effectively. Another key factor is that the CEO can be more creative, exploring new options and spending time on opportunities and productivity, rather than "process." The executive (CEO) can respond to board concerns in a more professional manner and is better positioned to interface with directors who are (or were) leaders in business organizations. There is no question that the non-profit executive president/CEO has operational authority.

2. The issue of flexibility. Reducing the board's involvement with operational issues means decisions can be made more quickly and efficiently. (Under the traditional system, thirty-five days or longer can easily pass while a minor issue is considered by a board committee, the full board, and then implemented by management.) Do remember to review corporate bylaws to make certain they do not have too many bureaucratic procedures.

3. The issue of efficiency. One very important benefit of the Model is that it helps reduce costs. No matter how conscientious the board member is, he or she needs some staff support to make decisions. Staff support is often costly because the nonprofit uses operational funds to bring volunteers up to date on operational issues well understood by its professional staff. The president/CEO should carefully monitor the amount of staff time that is devoted to providing board reports.

4. What are the Model's limitations? Maintaining board members' commitment is the largest issue. Personal gratification is more immediate for board members when they are working with operational rather than policy questions. Board members require ongoing attention from the CEO to heighten their motivation. (Note: this is especially true during the transition to the Model because the level of detail on agendas drops dramatically.) The president/CEO should meet with each director informally. Directors must have clear evidence that their efforts make a difference and that their time is being used wisely and (for board members who are professionals and businesspeople) economically. After implementation, some directors may grumble about the lack of immediate action items and may feel they are not making a good contribution with their time.

5. Assessment of CEO. Assessment must be fair and rigorous and conducted annually. Proper assessment is critical to the successful operation of the Corporate Model. The assessment process is especially crucial for nonprofits because the profit factor as a measurement of performance is absent. It is also critical that the president/CEO view the assessment process as fair.

6. Setting salaries of executive staff. The board sets only the president/CEO salary. He or she then sets all other staff salaries, within budget guidelines.

7. Avoiding end runs. Both board members and management need to agree that all personnel decisions are the responsibility of the president/CEO, except in instances where deception and discrimination are alleged and verified. If too many personnel problems arise, the issue should be reviewed in the CEO's assessment.

8. Importance of titles. The titles "CEO" and "president" signal clearly to the public who has the final authority in all operational matters and can speak for the organization. They are not ambiguous. The terms "manager" or "executive director" do not carry the same external clout. An executive director can be the administrator in a small church or the operational head of a large arts organization. The public and some corporate directors often view managers and executive directors (because of the organizational history of nonprofits) as "hired hands," not as managerial professionals who are able to handle all operational responsibilities.

9. The amount of trust required under the Corporate Model. The Model creates an entirely new working environment. It calls for a working relationship based on trust and mutual respect. All communications go through the CEO. He or she is the person accountable to the board and is the representative of the staff. This is why the assessment of the CEO must be thorough and why it is so critical to the success of the Corporate Model—"Trust but verify." This working environment is a new kind of "culture." It must involve a solid partnership between the board and staff. The president/CEO represents the staff on the board. Where allowed by state law, the president/CEO should be a voting member of the board, as a tangible *symbol* of the solid partnership. Jack stressed over and over this is a key ingredient in the Corporate Model. However, he also pointed to an Urban Institute study that reports, "If the CEO serves on the board, the board is less engaged, and it may undermine the board's stewardship role." Jack firmly believes that the board chair and the CEO must make certain that the board is fully engaged. Having the CEO as a board member makes him or her a peer, not a powerhouse.

10. Formality. Yes, it is more formal. But this is a natural outcome of any growing organization, whether it is a for-profit or nonprofit organization. Events, such as celebrations of program successes, need to be held to ensure that there is some interpersonal contact between board and staff.

From: Jack Billings
Sent: December 17 6:52 PM
To: Russ Peterson
Subject: Excellent recap!

Russ –

Re: your recap. It's great! Will be interested to hear from you after you share it with some of your fellow board members.

Here's something you'll want to know. I was talking to a friend of mine yesterday.

He's an executive director of a nonprofit group with an annual budget of $5 million. He estimates that his organization spends at least $50,000 a year in staff time to serve his board's various committees.

I suggested to him that the Corporate Model could cut these costs, because it eliminates or sharply reduces board involvement in operational matters.

Some cautionary thoughts: I hope I haven't made the process of switching to the Model sound too easy. You'll want to be certain your fellow directors at Yorkville realize that they will face the following problems:

- Making the switch is a touchy process.
- Tradition will probably hamper you all the way.
- Despite the fact the Corporate Model has been around for thirty-five years, the concept is still considered new and somewhat controversial.
- If you adopt it, you may be among the first nonprofits in the area to do so.
- Some board members will be afraid of losing control.
- Some staff may fear that your organization will become "too businesslike."

But what is most important is that your executive director has to be ready for the significant increase in responsibility. If an executive director is incapable of or unwilling to change, nothing can be done until the nonprofit gets a new exec. Since I am well acquainted with Joyce Thomas, Yorkville's executive director, I have a lot of confidence in her ability to change.

Jack

BTW: My own recap—I'm absolutely convinced that the Corporate Model makes it possible for a board to concentrate on the major policy issues before it. In turn, that means the organization is better able to serve its clients.

THE BOTTOM LINE IS: THE ADVANTAGES OF THE CORPORATE MODEL FAR OUTWEIGH THE DIFFICULTIES IN MAKING THE SWITCH.

"Dick is trying to make an end run on increasing his salary – it won't work under the Corporate Model"

3

HOW THE MODEL IS STRUCTURED

Intentional Simplicity

From: Jack Billings
Sent: January 4 6:12 AM
To: Russ Peterson
Subject: Our structure—three standing
           committees

Russ –

Last night I took time to quickly scan our recent
e-mail exchanges and realized that in the flurry
that always accompanies the end of the year, I'd
forgotten to send you a copy of my agency's organizational chart.

Some of your board colleagues will probably be
surprised at how uncluttered it is. The simplicity
is intentional.

Note that our structure provides for only three
standing committees—Executive, Planning and
Resource, and Assessment.

Executive Committee—consists of CEO, corporate officers, and an at-large member elected
by the board. The committee acts for the board
between meetings, subject to later board ratification; sets the monthly agenda; reviews reports
for board discussion; and appoints members to
all standing and *ad hoc* committees. Executive,
which usually meets monthly, is our most active

committee. (Boards of nonprofits whose members are in different locations—e.g., national groups—can have exec committee meetings monthly via conference call.) It is not uncommon for some people to become concerned about giving the Executive Committee too much power. In practice, however, committee members consult with others on particularly difficult decisions or if the committee is so evenly divided that the decision could go either way. I've yet to see a situation in which the Executive Committee has operated in an imprudent manner.

Planning and Resource Committee assists the CEO in long-range planning. (As CEO, I direct the long-range planning effort and am the person chiefly responsible for developing the vision of what the organization might become in the future, subject to the input of the staff and the input and approval of the board.) Because the board has only three committees, Planning & Resource clearly plays an important role, making it easier to keep strategic planning a prominent part of board agendas. As you have discovered all too well at Yorkville, this isn't always an easy task in the nonprofit arena.

Planning & Resource also monitors the activities of the ad hoc committees. All of our ad hoc committees are established for a specific purpose and then disbanded when their work is complete. For example, our nominating committee operates only when needed to fill board vacancies and to develop a slate of new officers.

Assessment Committee—along with the CEO, this committee develops the initial drafts of the organizational goals, subject to review by the Exec Committee and input and approval by the full board. The CEO also needs to make certain that communication between the Assessment and Planning/Resource committees is clear. Most of the goals are yearly ones; others cover a two- or three-year span. After the goals are established, this committee is responsible for an objective assessment of the CEO and the organization's performance. This assessment is based on goal attainment as well as on the detailed review of the fiscal audit completed by our external auditors. A subgroup of the Assessment Committee can act as a formal audit subcommittee since audit committee activities have become increasingly important in recent years. Recommendations made by the Assessment Committee are used to help establish goals for the following year and for the CEO's performance and salary evaluation.

Side note: Instead of having financial operations monitored by the Assessment Committee, some organizations choose to establish a separate Finance Committee. Based on my experience and observation, the decision to have such a committee should be based on two factors: the level of financial support needed by the CEO and the complexity of the organization's finances. If a Finance Committee is established, a subset of it can also serve as the audit committee and have overall responsibility for assessing the organization's financial health and meet with the external auditors to bring financial issues into sharper focus and, hopefully, to prevent fraud. (I should point out here that some states require all nonprofits to have a separately functioning audit committee.) Specifically, the Finance Committee would assume the following duties (all of which are Assessment Committee activities in my own organization):

- Work with the vice president of finance to review financial statements.
- Set policy on endowment investments, subject to board ratification.
- Meet, as needed, with the external auditors and the internal auditors if the organization is large enough to have them. These meetings should take place three or four times a year, at a minimum.
- Review the formal management letter.
- Review operations of financial policy.

- Function as an audit committee, assuming a separate audit committee is not established to meet state legal requirements.

In our nonprofit, we find these three standing committees are definitely sufficient. But there are others working in the nonprofit arena who make different suggestions. I'm aware of one expert who calls for these three committees: Internal Affairs, External Affairs, and Governance. I've also heard someone recommend there be five committees, consisting of Board Operations, Planning & Program Development, Performance Oversight & Monitoring, External Relations & Resource Development, and Audit.

Your board, if it adopts the Corporate Model, may want to add a Finance Committee or in some other ways vary our organization chart. Let me know what questions people there have after reviewing the attached information.

Jack

BTW: A note of caution—if you go too far beyond three standing committees, you run the risk of having what I call the "spaghetti factory" organizational chart.

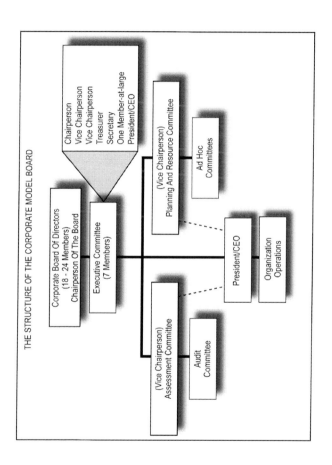

THE STRUCTURE OF THE CORPORATE MODEL BOARD

Corporate Board Of Directors
(18 - 24 Members)
Chairperson Of The Board

Executive Committee
(7 Members)

Chairperson
Vice Chairperson
Vice Chairperson
Treasurer
Secretary
One Member-at-large
President/CEO

(Vice Chairperson)
Planning And Resource Committee

Ad Hoc
Committees

(Vice Chairperson)
Assessment Committee

Audit
Committee

President/CEO

Organization
Operations

From: Russ Peterson
Sent: January 12 9:28 PM.
To: Jack Billings
Subject: Elite board? Can you avoid?

Jack,

I forwarded your e-mail and attachment (i.e., your organizational chart) and asked for reactions from some of my Yorkville board colleagues. The feedback I received leads me to pose four questions:

1) Why a board of eighteen to twenty-four members? (Our board has thirty members now.)

2) If we had to reduce the size of our board, how would we do it? (We want both expertise and experience on our board.)

3) How do you get by without a standing building committee? Personnel committee?

4) Are you, as president /CEO, a voting member of the board?

The people I've talked to on the Yorkville board are impressed with how efficient the Corporate Model appears on paper. Your organizational chart certainly reduces the layers of board governance and focuses on board responsibilities.

At the same time, we don't want a committee structure so streamlined that it creates an elite group of board members (those who really know what's going on) and leaves the rest of the board to merely rubber stamp decisions. We want to be sure we would not sacrifice board teamwork just for the sake of simplicity.

Russ

From: Jack Billings
Sent: January 15 7:42 PM
To: Russ Peterson
Subject: Effective board governance—it
           matters!

Russ –

We've been hit with a tremendous snowstorm. Can't get anywhere this morning. Gives me an unexpected opportunity to answer your e-mail and relax at home with an extra cup of coffee.

Before tackling your questions, I'd like to comment on something you said in your last e-mail. Your Yorkville colleagues are impressed with how the organizational chart I sent you "reduces the layers of board governance." What the Corporate Model really does is eliminate some board activity that is better handled by management. I'm not nitpicking here. I want to make an important point and, at the same time, pave the way for answering your questions.

The Corporate Model is based on the premise that good management is not the same as good board governance. A second key concept is that you can't have one without the other. In other words, to improve the leadership and effectiveness of management you must make board governance more effective.

The organizational plan I sent was adopted here with these concepts in mind. Keeping them in focus, let me go on to answer your questions.

1) If you look at the number of board members on other nonprofit boards, you'll find that eighteen to twenty-five members is a workable number. (The national median in 2010 was seventeen, as reported by Board Source, with fifteen to twenty-two being the "sweet spot.") I have seen some with ten to twelve members and excellent performance records and others with large boards of about fifty members that just seemed unmanageable. The crucial thing is not how big the board is, but whether it works. Ours does. It's a workable group because the number is manageable. Also, remember that under the Corporate Model your board wouldn't be staffing a lot of committees that discuss issues already reviewed by staff.

2) From our experience here, I recommend that if you adopt the Model, you pare down the size of your board. You can do that gradually. As terms end, do not refill

them. You will find some people will leave automatically. Be prepared, however, for one or two directors to leave with some ill feelings. Depending on what you have for a term-of-service pattern, the downsizing may be more difficult than we had here. Recognize that there may be short time periods when diversity may be out of balance or certain skills in short supply. Also you may have to carefully stoke some egos. Asking some board members to become honorary directors, with the ability to attend meetings, may be helpful. Board members who are particularly interested in hands-on involvement may opt to serve in a different volunteer capacity within the organization. You don't have to necessarily sacrifice expertise or experience, but the makeup of the board will inevitably change. That's OK. It's even healthy.

3) We get by without a standing personnel committee (or building committee or others you could name) by appointing ad hoc committees as needed. For example, we don't need a standing personnel committee, because the ongoing personnel issues (e.g., hiring, firing, promotions) are the responsibility of management. However, If we want to determine whether to

change our pension plan (a major policy issue), we appoint a board committee to work with staff to investigate the alternatives. When its work is completed, the committee is disbanded.

4) As president/CEO, I am a voting member of our board, which is something that is allowed by our state charter. (Nationally the 2010 proportion of president/CEO's who were voting members was fifteen percent, as reported by Board Source.) Our board took this voting route for symbolic purposes—to put the top manager who represents the staff on the same level as the volunteer board. Tell your colleagues that I've never cast the deciding vote in the four years we've worked under the Model. Nor have I heard of another CEO being put in this position. The power to vote makes you a peer, not a powerhouse.

Jack

P.S. We don't have an elite group of board members who run the show. What we have is an active board. Every member does work that is valuable to the organization and meetings are held for specific purposes. Most of my board members have what I call time-compressed lifestyles.

They appreciate limiting their board activities to what's important and specific.

BTW: Reducing the number of board members is not as unusual as you may think. Many non-profits with boards of fifty or sixty or more—numbers that are not uncommon for national associations—have found large boards to be expensive and unwieldy. Having a large board also tends to consolidate power in the hands of a few committee people. I once belonged to a national professional association that had one hundred ten board members—who together represented four significant groups of stakeholders. Costs of board meetings were staggering. Yet, over a five-year period, we were able to reduce the number to forty. Believe me, it was impossible to have a discussion with one hundred ten people, but with forty it is a little more manageable.

Hey, it FINALLY stopped snowing. Time to shovel!

From: Russ Peterson
Sent: January 21 11:30 PM.
To: Jack Billings
Subject: Now we're serious

Jack,

What a night! Thought I'd dash off a quick message despite the hour just to tell you to keep your
e-mails coming!

Tonight, at my suggestion, the Yorkville board
voted to appoint a committee to review our present structure and determine whether we need to
make some changes. I've been appointed, along
with five other board members, to investigate options for the future.

In my recent e-mails, I've been so interested in
getting information about the Model that I've ne-
glected to tell you about the growing frustration
of the board. Tonight, after a particularly long
discussion on minor issues, I couldn't restrain
myself any longer. I pointed out that because
we're so mired in operational issues we haven't
tackled major policy or long-range planning issues for more than six months. Believe me that
comment opened up some lively discussion! It
was obvious the time had come for this board to
look at its future.

Our first committee meeting is next week. I'm ready for it. I want this committee to seriously consider the Corporate Model. Be prepared. I know there will be questions. I appreciate your continuing interest.

Russ

From: Jack Billings
Sent: January 22 7:54 AM
To: Russ Peterson
Subject: I'm ready for your questions!

Russ –

Fire questions at me as they come!

By now you realize just how completely I support the Corporate Model. I look forward to helping you determine whether it is an answer for Yorkville. First, though, some quick thoughts:

As I've indicated before, be aware that some board members and staff will look at the Model as "an insensitive business approach." You'll probably find these people (particularly staff) fearful that management will become cold, distant, and unfeeling. My contention is that you can have a big heart and still have good management.

Don't underestimate potential concerns about board members' involvement. Be aware that old culture can create "drag" when it comes to implementing change.

Handling policy and strategy issues simply isn't as immediately rewarding and personally interesting as handling operational issues. The CEO needs to allocate more time for meeting with individual directors and try to respond to any and all directors, as needed, more personally. However, there are ways to make sure board members' involvement is truly meaningful and satisfying. Down the road, I'll give you more pointers in this area.

For now, good luck with that first committee meeting.

I hope the rest of the committee is as committed as you are to finding a better way for Yorkville.

Jack

BTW: If you review our e-mails, you'll see we've come a long way in a short time. We've discussed the need for changing nonprofit board structures as well as the efficiency and effectiveness underlying the Corporate Model. We've also covered a synopsis of the Model's working structure.

YOU'VE GOT THE OUTLINE. FROM THIS POINT ON, WE NEED TO ELABORATE ON THE PARTS OF THE MODEL. THE PARTS ARE CRITICAL, PARTICULARLY THE OPERATION AND PRODUCTIVITY OF THE ASSESSMENT COMMITTEE.

4

ASSESSMENT AND THE MODEL

The CEO Cannot Be Insecure

From: Russ Peterson
Sent: January 29 10:41 PM
To: Jack Billings
Subject: Assessment—need to know more

Jack,

The six of us who were appointed to look at the structure of the Yorkville board met for the first time tonight. It was a productive session, with each committee member agreeing to take on a specific assignment.

As you might have guessed, I'm in charge of bringing in as much information as possible on the Corporate Model. We had time for only a brief discussion, but once again, I find that you're right on target. Initial questions are focused on the whole issue of assessment.

Any thoughts, guidance, or direction you can give me in this area will be useful.

Russ

From: Jack Billings
Sent: January 31 5:21 PM
To: Russ Peterson
Subject: Assessment—need to know more
Attachment: Fred Jackson comments.pdf

Russ –

Last spring I was one of several speakers at a large national meeting. I spoke at length on the structure and inner workings of the Corporate Model. Two people who followed me on the platform made some interesting comments about "living with the Model."

The first one, Fred Jackson, is the top executive of a human service agency in New York State. The other, Sarah Tobin, is the head of a non-profit trade association in the Midwest. Luckily, a friend of mine taped most of that session, and I have almost all of their comments. I'm enclosing excerpts from Fred's speech, roughly transcribed by my administrative assistant. I must have given my copy of Sarah's comments to someone but will forward them when my assistant is back from vacation in a few days. The information should be pertinent to your investigation.

Jack

BTW: Fred Jackson's NY nonprofit has been operating under the Corporate Model for eight years.

Living with the Model
Comments by Fred Jackson

A lot of people aren't quite comfortable with the whole concept of assessment. It scares them. It can be particularly upsetting in the nonprofit world because organizational outcomes are very often measured "qualitatively" rather than "quantitatively." Quite often, I've found executive directors and CEOs don't really understand how boards determine goals and expected outcomes because they don't work with their boards in establishing them. Let me illustrate my point with a story.

Last month I was in Detroit with the chairman of my board of directors, giving a workshop on the Corporate Model to executives and board members. Eight of the twenty workshop participants were senior executives (some EDs, others presidents/CEOs) from various nonprofit agencies, ranging from a developmental center to an automotive trade association. They happened to be sitting near each other in the center of the room, which made it easy for me to see all of their faces when I began sharing the assessment report completed a few weeks earlier by my board. Included in the report was the board's evaluation of my performance.

Twenty minutes into my presentation it was obvious that all eight of the executives were totally surprised, you might say aghast, at my candor.

"Fred, do you really want this information, including some criticisms of your own performance, to get out?" I was asked. "Certainly," I said. "It's already public knowledge, and public policy now requires all of us to become more transparent."

"Are you also comfortable knowing your board members are out inquiring about your performance—asking how Fred Jackson is doing?"

"Not only am I comfortable with it, but I also expect it," I answered. "The people doing the inquiring are members of my board's Assessment Committee doing their job. They need to talk to others to determine how I am doing and how the organization is doing."

Looking around the room, I noticed that the other twelve workshop participants in the room—mostly board members from various other Detroit non-profit organizations—were also surprised by my comments.

"The president/CEO of a nonprofit organization cannot be an insecure person," I said. "If I live in fear that I'll lose my job, I won't accomplish anything."

I told that group, and repeat here today, that I believe the most important job of the board of a nonprofit is to find the best possible person to manage the organization, then stand back and let that person manage.

In turn, the most important job of the top staff person in any nonprofit is to manage to the very best of his or her ability, then stand back and allow one's management performance to be thoroughly evaluated.

The assessment process does not mean that Fred Jackson, president and CEO, has to have an adversarial relationship with his board. I expect to be involved with the evaluation planning process as the committee develops it. The directors of a nonprofit organization and the head of that organization are on the same team. However, like virtually any other kind of team, its members have different roles and responsibilities.

At the beginning of every year, directors on the Assessment Committee and the nonprofit's top staff person agree on joint goals for the organization and their measurement. These goals, which the entire board must ratify, should be achievable but challenging. Because of the nature of nonprofits, some goals can be measured only in qualitative terms. To the extent possible, however, the goals set should be ones you can quantify, despite the fact that board and managers will agree some measures are imperfect.

For example, in my own nonprofit we agree that the metrics on clients served are verifiable, but metrics on our community impact are imperfect—that is, they are developed from small samples, or are anecdotal, subjective, interpretive, or qualitative. But we simply can't spend tens of thousands or hundreds of thousands of dollars to have an outside consultant provide statistically solid community impact outcome metrics. However, you won't be surprised to hear that the accounting outcome data used in assessments are never viewed as *imperfect* measures!

On my own board, assessment is very thorough and takes place annually. That doesn't mean it's done all at one time. Assessment occurs throughout the year, depending on how Assessment Committee members decide to divide their tasks.

After completing its entire investigation, the Assessment Committee makes its report to our board. It doesn't have to be done this way. I know of some Corporate Model boards where assessment updates are given periodically throughout the year.

The CEO has to understand that the full board must make some subjective judgments based on the Assessment Committee's findings. The CEO must be strong enough to live with these judgments, because under the Corporate Model, the CEO is told what the board wants but not how to achieve it. Hopefully, the CEO is involved in developing the "rules" for making the judgments.

I might add here that the CEO must also be strong enough to handle criticism. The CEO is going to be criticized—that happens in every creative, dynamic organization. What upsets some managers is that the criticism is made public in a written report. We must remind ourselves that all of us need to recognize the need to improve our performances in some ways.

You might ask, "Who would want such a job?" After many years with the Model, I can honestly say, "I like working this way!"

As the president and CEO under the Model, I can be far more creative than the typical manager of a traditional nonprofit organization. My responsibility is to live within the mission, budget, and guidelines set by the board. My board doesn't get involved with how many computer disks, room dividers, or paper clips I buy. I don't have to go to the board for each contract negotiated during the year. I don't get locked into endless discussion about personnel issues.

The community knows the organization and Fred Jackson are on the move.

Assessment is a report card. It tells me, the board, and the community how well the organization is doing what it set out to do.

From: Jack Billings
Sent: February 1 5:22 PM.
To: Russ Peterson
Subject: Assessment—second story
Attachment: Sarah Tobin comments.pdf

Russ-

I got lucky and found in the middle of a long string of old e-mails, an electronic copy of Sarah Tobin's speech, which it turns out, I had asked her to forward to me. She heads a nonprofit trade association in Missouri.

Jack

Life Under the Corporate Model
Comments by Sarah Tobin

I was a true skeptic. As far as I was concerned, the Corporate Model was nothing more than an ego trip for the executive. When I was asked by my board to consider it, I remember thinking, "How can restructuring and new titles help? If we need to fix something, just tell me what it is and I'll work harder for a few more hours and take care of it."

At the urging of my board, I reluctantly agreed to accept the Model. Three years have passed since then, and one-time skeptic Sarah Tobin can now stand before you and tell you that the Model has indeed changed the very nature of our organization. Take, for instance, my own position.

It is probably easier for the board to fire me. Heretofore, when so many operational matters were "shared decisions," the outcomes were also a shared responsibility. If something went wrong, I shared the blame. Now, if something goes wrong, it takes no guesswork to figure who is responsible.

Within the first few weeks after my board made the switch, I realized that if I weren't mature enough to accept that level of responsibility and accountability, I probably did not deserve my job. I told myself, "If I can't stand that much heat, I'd better not stand on the launch pad."

Actually, the Model has reduced the "heat" I feel, which never was oppressive. Now I have more flexibility, more freedom to act, and waste less time and motion. I'm not providing a group of decision makers with enough information so that they can come to the same conclusion I had reached.

In summary, I've been empowered to do my job. What my board wants from me are results that can be fairly measured by means of quantitative or qualitative methods. No question qualitative information is open to broad interpretation. However, using and improving imperfect metrics over time can fairly track progress and drive positive change for the organization. That's where I must rely on those making the assessment to demonstrate they are reasonable individuals making fair (not perfect) judgments.

Joint operational decision making between board and staff (and board micromanagement) may help everyone feel busy and involved, but unfortunately, it may involve people in the wrong things and fail to use their talents in the most effective way. I think more carefully now about my decisions, but knowing that they are mine and that I am trusted with the authority to make them is a blessing. I have discovered that these new arrangements are invigorating and do not bring about more "heat."

From: Russ Peterson
Sent: February 4 5:07 PM
To: Jack Billings
Subject: How do you set up Assessment
            Committee?

Jack,

A number of comments in the two speeches you
sent gave me real insight into the role of the
CEO, the critical importance of assessment, and
the value of assessment for the organization.

What I need now is some basic information about
how to set up an Assessment Committee.

Russ

From: Jack Billings
Sent: February 6 7:41 PM
To: Russ Peterson
Subject: Assessment Committee—step by step

Russ –

Typically, seven to nine of a board's twenty to twenty-five directors make up the Assessment Committee. Members are appointed by the board's Executive Committee. (The president/CEO is not a voting member of the Assessment Committee but attends most sessions, as he or she does with the Planning & Resource Committee.) The individuals appointed must be willing to confront hard issues and make recommendations. They must be conscientious and thorough.

The first order of business is to work with the president/CEO to establish both personal goals for the president/CEO and program goals for the organization. These are developed from lists compiled by the president/CEO and the Assessment Committee chairperson.

Next, the committee maps out its agenda and work schedule over time. At Yorkville, for example, your committee might decide to assess an established "wellness program" every two years but choose to evaluate a new staff-development program at the end of each of the next three years. Obviously, fiscal goals are monitored each month and evaluated closely every year. The president/CEO's personal goals are usually evaluated annually.

The committee chairperson assigns individual tasks for the year. This work can be done easily if it is divided fairly among members. Usually, individual tasks take each person a total of one or two days a year, plus a few meetings with the entire committee.

Each person on the committee takes the steps necessary to get the data he or she needs (for example, from internal data or interviews with staff, interviews in the community, or surveys). Each person then prepares a four- to eight-page written report. A typical program or project assessment report will include the following:

- a brief history
- a summary of goals and objectives
- a list of staff, organization, and facilities
- budget (including funding source and trends)
- assessment of strengths, areas in need of improvement, continuing appropriateness and recommendations.

- the president/CEO's annual performance goals
- recommendations

The full committee does not need numerous meetings throughout the year. The committee chairperson's job is to make sure things get done as scheduled. The chairperson also coordinates the various written reports and sends periodic updates on the committee's work to the full board.

Several times a year (or more, if needed) the entire Assessment Committee or a subcommittee of it meet, as a corporate Audit Committee, with the organization's external auditors. Part of each meeting is held in executive session, which is one of the few times that management is excluded from any meeting.

Management understands that this procedure does not reflect on the integrity of the management group. In fact, when the Assessment Committee is initially established, this process should be presented as standard procedure because it has become more common for both business and nonprofit boards—resulting from various for-profit and not-for-profit board debacles that were well publicized in the past decade.

Typical questions asked during the executive session are:

- Did you notice any unusual transactions, unusual travel/entertainment expenses, or other large payments?
- Was management cooperative during the audit?
- Is there anything else you want to tell us in the absence of management?

In the business world, these questions are asked by board audit committees. Many large accounting firms provide complimentary booklets describing how audit committees operate. You might want to obtain one of these booklets as a guide to determining the procedure for your Assessment Committee.

At the end of the year, the full committee reviews all committee reports and financial reports. It then summarizes these reports and submits its final document to the full board. This final report includes an assessment of the president/CEO based on the overall findings of the committee.

Given this recap, do you have any other questions about assessment?

Jack

P.S. I hear your high school senior has applied to my son's college. Do you think Paul will go there?

From: Russ Peterson
Sent: February 12 12:06 PM
To: Jack Billings
Subject: What if Assessment Committee falls
          short?

Jack,

I do have one more question. What if the
Assessment Committee doesn't do its work well?

Seems to me, if that happened, your system of
checks and balances fails. The organization
could end up being run more for the staff than for
the people it is supposed to benefit. Management
could run wild in setting salaries or fees or fail to
deliver a quality product.

I'm sure you remember the big scandal at the
United Way of America's national office a number of years ago. Seems to me, there were serious issues involving people at the highest levels
in the organization. Scandals, in fact, seem to be
everyday occurrences. Here's a recent example
from my own hometown—the bookkeeper for an
amateur hockey association embezzled $934,000
from a pool of money that had been raised to
build a rink!

Russ

BTW: Paul is waiting anxiously for college acceptance letters. His first choice is your son's school.

From: Jack Billings
Sent: February 15 5:46 PM
To: Russ Peterson
Subject: Be serious about fraud protection

Russ –

I was wondering if you would ask me about that
notorious scandal at United Way in connection
with the issue of proper Assessment! Virtually
everyone involved with nonprofits (or more correctly, everyone who has been around nonprofits for a while) remembers this scandal because
the top executive's salary was so generous and
the perks so extensive. You may recall charges
of fraud and conspiracy were filed against top
United Way managers.

In my opinion, the United Way scandal and the
hockey rink story you cited are dramatic examples of what potentially can happen if management has no checks and balances. Management,
as you so aptly put it, can run wild. Remember
though, the potential for self-serving behavior
exists regardless of how an organization is structured. I assume you have read articles about companies whose managers establish highly lucrative
bonus plans ("golden parachutes") in case their
firms are purchased by or merged with another
organization. A nonprofit's management team

under the Corporate Model is not likely to run wild, however, for the following reasons:

From day one, any nonprofit organization that adopts the Corporate Model also has to be committed to the idea of rigorous assessment, conducted annually. The board must determine whether there are any problems with the Assessment Committee and move as quickly as possible to correct them.

It has been my observation, and the observation of others, that the Model helps nonprofits build a cadre of superior managers.

Many nonprofits are evaluated by outside accrediting or review organizations, which also ascertain whether the nonprofit is benefiting client groups. This information helps to supplement a reasonable, although not perfect, system of checks and balances provided through the work of the Assessment Committee.

While fraud may be difficult to detect, there are seven actions a Corporate Model board should take, alerting all interested observers to the fact that board members are giving serious attention to fraud protection. Hopefully, these actions will deter someone from trying to steal from the organization.

1) Check the adequacy of internal control: make certain that accounting and control systems are divided into operating functions performed by different staff members who check each other's work.

2) Obtain certification from the external auditors that governance records and financial records are in place and in proper form.

3) Require proper authorization of activities and expenditures: direct staff to provide two signatures for certain expenditures.

4) Determine existence of physical assets: request that major physical assets be inspected visually by the external auditors.

5) Review the nonprofit's tax-exempt status and identify any activities that may endanger the nonprofit (this activity should be part of the annual certification conducted by the external auditor).

6) Ascertain whether payroll taxes, license fees, and sales taxes are promptly paid and corporate reports are filed in a timely manner: the external auditor needs to review documentation in such areas with great care.

7) Change auditing firms, or the partner in change of the account, every three to five years.

8) Make certain all persons with access to cash are covered by a bond, policy.

Jack

BTW: I should tell you what happened at United Way in the wake of that scandal. The board addressed the situation by revising audit committee procedures and adding an outside advisory committee for the audit committee.

From: Jack Billings
Sent: February 15 5:58 PM
To: Russ Peterson
Subject: An outline of Assessment process
Attachment: Outline -Assessment process.pdf.

Russ –

I was about ready to shut down my computer and go home, when I realized I had something else available to help your committee with its work. It is an outline showing how one organization, which has had a lot of experience with the Model, handles its assessment process. Use it as a guide (my own organization found it very helpful) and feel free to adapt it to meet your own board's needs. For example, the outline shows how the initial negotiations on goals can be handled by the chair of the Assessment Committee or the board chairperson. In your case, you may want the board chair to take on this assignment.

THE ASSESSMENT PROCESS

How Evaluation is Accomplished
• Joint Goal Setting
-    Begins with CEO, using past year as base
-    CEO negotiates upcoming year's goals with board chairperson or Assessment Committee chair

- CEO and Chairperson or Assessment Chair complete revisions
- Executive Committee reviews goals
- Executive Committee sets timeframe (one to three years for individual goals)

• Assessment Committee Evaluation Process
- Committee determines appropriate times for evaluation
- Assessment chairperson coordinates
- Committee members interview / analyze data, etc. (time commitment for this task is six to eight hours a year for each committee member)
- Each person writes section of assessment report
- Chairperson compiles report
- Committee reviews full draft
- Committee sends report to Executive Committee for comment
- Assessment Committee meets with external auditors
- Executive Committee sends report to the full board

• The Assessment Committee Report
Can be as long as fifty pages, or if really needed up to one hundred pages, with each section containing:

- Brief history
- Summary of goals and objectives
- Staff, organization, and facilities
- Budget (funding sources and trends)
- Strengths
- Needed improvements
- Continuing concerns
- Recommendations

Basic Principles of Evaluation

- Rigorous assessment of the CEO and the organization are necessary to ensure the organization's future.
- The assessment process clearly establishes executive authority and responsibility.
- All nonprofit groups need to allow for management flexibility and creativity.
- The management team requires latitude for risk taking because inevitably some projects will fail.
- Evaluation is designed to assess outcomes of policy implementation, not how operations took place.
- The focus is on productivity and outcomes.
- Evaluation can highlight the need for policy change.
- Board understands no executive performs perfectly.

- The assessment team must be reasonable and fair-minded.
- Assessment is not adversarial in practice or spirit.
- Evaluation is an on-going process.

From: Jack Billings
Sent: February 17 6:18 PM
To: Russ Peterson
Subject: Legal issues + expanded Form 990

Russ –

I was talking to our board chair yesterday and told her about our e-mail exchanges. She asked if I'd remembered to mention the board's obligation re: "reputational risk," a couple of legal issues, and the expanded 990 Form that need to be considered during the assessment process. Have to admit, I'd forgotten, but I can quickly catch you up on the topic of reputational risk, plus she e-mailed me information to pass on to you regarding her other points.

Reputational risk is shorthand for saying that management and the board must plan to protect legally the organization's reputation, especially when a minor internal problem can become well known in the community. Bottom line: a small unfortunate incident, if poorly handled, can damage the organization's reputation and seriously impact fund development.

BTW: my board chair is not a lawyer, so regarding the material below, she asked me to tell you it is being sent as information, not as legal advice.

I've cut and pasted key information from her e-mail about the Intermediate Sanctions Act, which applies to nonprofit organizations; the Sarbanes-Oxley Act, which some nonprofits adhere to (or at least adhere to certain provisions of) even though it was not written to cover nonprofits; and the required enhanced Form 990.

Intermediate Sanctions Act—passed by Congress in the late 1990s
(Covered by Section 4958 of the IRS Code)

This act applies to nonprofit organizations. As I understand it, the act states that any volunteer, manager, or director who receives an *excess benefit*, is liable to be billed by the IRS for an excise tax on the excess benefit received. That means, for example, if a nonprofit sells land with an apprised market value of $100K to a volunteer for $75K, the IRS could levy personal excise taxes on managers and directors who approved the excess benefit transaction. The same type of tax penalty could be levied on a CEO and individual directors if a board approved an excess salary for the CEO, i.e., one above the market rate for the position. (If you are interested in the details, Section 4958 of the IRS Code provides information on the taxes that might be levied). Prior to passage of this act, the only action that the IRS could take in these types of situations would have been revocation of the nonprofit's tax-exempt status (which, of course, could negatively impact innocent clients of the nonprofit.)

My board chair's comment about the Intermediate Sanctions Act: "I'm often surprised how many nonprofit executives and tax advisors are not aware this act exists!"

Sarbanes-Oxley Act—passed by Congress in 2002

Sarbanes-Oxley or SOX covers publicly traded corporations, but NOT nonprofit organizations. I wanted to mention it because:

- some nonprofit boards have taken the costly step of voluntarily following its provisions;
- some nonprofits maintain that state disclosure laws and required forms (Form 990 or 990-PF) provide enough public financial information;
- other nonprofits maintain that the CEO and CFO need, at a minimum, to certify that the annual financial statements are correct (a key provision of Sarbanes-Oxley).

Russ, if the Yorkville board hasn't discussed these two acts, I suggest you might want to have a talk with your legal counsel.

The expanded Form 990—required by the IRS, took effect in 2009

Nonprofit governance is now high on the list of IRS interest areas, spurred largely by some highly publicized exempt organization governance failures. The IRS Form 990 report now includes twenty-eight governance questions related to the size and independence of nonprofit boards (i.e., issues related to governance, policies, and disclosures). The expanded report is designed to increase "transparency" for nonprofits. (Those who view it less kindly, such as my CFO when he's working his way through it, would describe it as a heck of an example of the increased compliance level now required of nonprofits!) From my board chair's perspective these expanded reports, at least from what she's reading now, appear to be helping board members get a broader view of their own organizations. She and I have both heard that some agencies expect to use their expanded Form 990s as public relations vehicles. That's not an unexpected response, we think, since almost all of the additional questions on the Form 990 have no right or wrong answer from a legal perspective, so organizations will strive to respond in ways that demonstrate they are well-governed entities.

But boards should also know that as part of stepped-up attention on nonprofits, the IRS now mandates that a governance checklist be completed by its revenue agents whenever they examine a 501(c)(3) organization. The checklist consists of twenty-eight questions and a four-page set of instructions for the agent. Lots of those questions mirror what's on the expanded Form 990, but the checklist delves deeper. Below are some of the key areas where a nonprofit can expect to be questioned, if examined, that I have abstracted from a talk by an IRS official:

- Does the nonprofit have a written mission statement that reflects its current purpose as a 501(c)(3)? If you have no mission statement, or one that is not aligned with current activities, you end up with a "no" on the agent's checklist.
- To whom do you provide the organization's articles and bylaws? How large is the governing body? Do your bylaws have requirements as to the board's composition, duties, qualifications, and voting rights? How often did a quorum of the board meet during the year? How often did the full board meet? Did the number

of meetings meet/exceed bylaw requirements? Does a single person or a select
few individuals effectively control the
organization? The answer is "yes" if the
board typically defers to a small group
or an individual on the board (certainly a subjective question for an agent to
answer!).

- In addition to more standard questions
(e.g., written conflict of interest policy) are business and family relationships among board members disclosed?
Disclosures required annually, the agent
will ask if nonprofit policy addresses re-
cusals, if actual conflicts were disclosed,
and if the organization's policy was ad-
hered to.

- There will also be questions about policies and procedures designed to assure
that assets are used in accord with the organization's mission, as well as questions
like these: How often did board members
get written reports on financial activities? How often were finances discussed?
Was an independent accountant's report
issued? Was it discussed by the board?
Was a management letter issued? Was it
reviewed by the board or a committee?
Were any of the accountant's recommendations adopted?

- Finally the agent will have to answer whether the examination was hindered by a lack of needed information.

Hope this is helpful!

Jack

BTW: Some additional thoughts about transparency—what really seems required of all nonprofits in the twenty-first century is to:

- Have an up-to-date Web site outlining basic financial, strategy, and outcome information.
- List names of key personnel and describe their responsibilities on your Web site.
- Post a copy of your IRS letter of determination on your Web site.

(Electronic dashboards are also beginning to take hold. In industry, business firms are using electronic dashboards successfully to leverage real-time analytics and make better decisions on the plant floor and throughout the enterprise. In the nonprofit world, organizations that are more sophisticated are now using electronic dashboards that provide a wide range of current information in order to deliver integrated performance data for management.)

Bottom line, while transparency aids assessment, what's critical to remember is that assessment has to be more thorough in a nonprofit than it is in a for-profit organization. Without shareholders, profits, and customers who can make choices, measurement of results is much more difficult.

If your committee at Yorkville ultimately recommends that the Corporate Model be adopted, it must also stress the role of assessment.

PROPER ASSESSMENT IS THE KEYSTONE— THE VERY HEART—OF THE MODEL.

5

THE MODEL AND THE FUTURE

The Planning and Resource Committee

From: Russ Peterson
Sent: February 21 6:42 AM.
To: Jack Billings
Subject: You are right about nostalgia

Jack,

Thanks for the heads up on Intermediate Sanctions and Sarbanes-Oxley. We have scheduled a review with our attorney. Fortunately, I was involved in submitting Yorkville's latest Form 990 and am aware of the governance issues raised.

So let me update you on where we stand now. My committee is really forging ahead. We held two committee sessions this week, and, at this point, no one still thinks we can salvage our current structure. The three committee members who've been investigating current board functions came back with a very critical report. They had interviewed Yorkville's key staff people, from Joyce Thomas on down, plus all members of the board's Executive Committee.

Joyce was very candid, as were her four top staff, and all of the Executive Committee members. The message is clear. We have no firm sense of where Yorkville is headed. In particular, its long-term financial stability is a matter of real concern. Joyce wants to spend more time managing and less time reporting to the Yorkville board and its committees. The Executive Committee recognizes the need to devote more time to planning.

However, as you predicted, a few influential board veterans just don't buy the idea that the board should set policy and leave operations entirely to management. One socially prominent individual even argued that the minivan vs. SUV debate was just the type of decision on which we could add value. It is strange, but most of the directors who question changing the status quo have backgrounds working in nonprofits. They argue that we have to know the operational details if we're to help Joyce achieve the agency's mission. After all, they told our interviewers, her early experience was in counseling, she took five years off to raise twins and help care for a dying parent. However, we did get agreement that Joyce, despite her "limitations," has been quite visionary and had been at the top of the nonprofit graduate management class she took three years ago at Wharton. Her professor there invites her to lecture to his class a couple of times a year!

Some of these board veterans are nostalgic about how things used to be when Yorkville was a small organization. As you warned me, some even fear that if they give up their role in helping run things around here, Yorkville will no longer be the caring organization it's known to be! It's obvious we're going to face a touchy situation with a few directors. I may be calling you for advice if we find things getting too hot!

On our small committee, I sense a growing interest in the Corporate Model as an alternative. And that brings me to my next request. In one of our conversations at Thanksgiving, you mentioned that the work of the Planning and Resource Committee is every bit as important as that of the Assessment Committee. What more can you tell me?

Russ

From: Jack Billings
Sent: February 23 6:49 AM
To: Russ Peterson
Subject: Your radar & traffic cop

Russ –

Simply stated, strategic and tactical planning are your lifelines. If planning is incomplete or otherwise inadequate, you may jeopardize the future of your organization.

Under the Model, the CEO is the person chiefly responsible for planning. The job of the Planning and Resource Committee is to assist the CEO in short-term and long-range planning. That may sound like a minor supportive role, but believe me, it isn't.

As you know, in the case of human service organizations, board members represent the community. With trade or professional organizations, the board represents the membership. The board has the primary responsibility for ensuring that the programs and services a nonprofit organization offers are in the best interest of the clients it serves and the community or membership it represents.

Specifically, the Planning and Resource Committee provides the "radar" for the board. It also acts as its "traffic cop." It provides the radar by evaluating whether the organization is being correctly positioned to meet the future needs of clients. (The roughly equivalent function in the for-profit world would be marketing research.) As traffic cop, it helps make certain that board projects align with the mission, are completed in a timely manner, and that wise use is made of volunteers' efforts and time.

The committee has an obligation to seek the best sources of information for policy changes and to review and filter changes that come before it. As you know, the staff, board, volunteers, and community members can initiate policy changes. The overall board is responsible for monitoring the implementation of adopted changes, which should be those that best fit the organization's mission, vision, values, and resources.

The members of this committee, more than any other, work closely with the organization's staff. The staff provides much of the background information necessary for the committee's work. Recently, for example, my own organization considered whether our program should expand outside our traditional service area. The Planning and Resource Committee's job was to investigate.

Four committee members met with various key staff members who would be involved in any expansion effort. Committee members and staff decided together how to proceed. Staff members then completed most of the actual background work. The product was a joint board/staff report that is now before our full board. At the same time, a second Planning and Resource subcommittee was working with staff to determine whether we should develop twenty-four-hour access for a number of our client services.

Over the course of a year, the Planning and Resource Committee is likely to complete a number of specific reports, which are then reviewed by the Executive Committee and finally by the full board. That means many people consider, discuss, and evaluate an issue before the entire board votes.

The chairperson of Planning and Resource coordinates the committee's work, and then updates the full board on its activities at each regular monthly board meeting.

Jack

BTW: I've got a call in to a colleague whose organization has used the Model twice as long as my organization has used it. I'll ask him if he can add to what I've told you. He's due back soon from vacation. Will write again after I've heard from him.

From: Jack Billings
Sent: February 28 8:47 PM
To: Russ Peterson
Subject: My colleague's input

Russ –

I finally caught up by phone with the colleague I mentioned in my last e-mail, the one who is a real veteran of the Corporate Model. He believes the Model's structure has allowed his nonprofit organization to move smoothly through a period of growth. When the Model was adopted nine years ago, his nonprofit had a $2 million budget, a staff of forty, and three offices. Today, he oversees a budget of $4.5 million and a staff of one hundred working in twelve locations.

If his board hadn't switched to the Model he doubts the organization would be where it is today. Board emphasis on policy making and planning was needed in order for the nonprofit to grow. He gives a great deal of credit to the efforts of his various Planning and Resource Committee members over the years.

The locations of the nine newest branch offices and the dates they were opened were critically important for his nonprofit, because initial start-up costs were unusually high for the kinds of services they provide (e.g., enriched assisted housing in apartment buildings so the elderly can age in place rather than being required to enter nursing homes). He said his Planning and Resource members did a tremendous job reviewing data provided by his staff. Committee members made valuable suggestions regarding the apartment complexes where they were considering locating enriched housing, and actively participated in making final recommendations that ultimately went to his full board.

In his experience, the decisions his full board makes usually follow the recommendations made in joint reports from Planning and Resource Committee members and staff. My colleague says that to date his nonprofit has been ahead of the competition in offering services.

He also noted that Planning and Resource Committee members on his board were responsible for developing a major five-year long-range planning report and that they update it annually. (BTW: here's one place where there are direct parallels with what often happens in the for-profit world.) Long-range-planning documents entail considerable staff time, he said, but they are well worth it in the end. He told me more about specific projects, but I think what I've told you so far gives you an idea of how critical a role Planning and Resource Committee members play.

It goes almost without saying, I think, that the interaction between staff and board committee members contributes significantly to the creativity within an organization.

Jack

From: Russ Peterson
Sent: March 5 12:30 PM
To: Jack Billings
Subject: Four very basic questions

Jack,

I appreciate how the Corporate Model gives an
organization the structure it needs to grow and
how it contributes to creativity at all levels. But
I still have a few very basic questions:

1. Can you give me some guidelines on setting
   up a Planning and Resource Committee?
2. How often would such a committee meet?
3. Is the CEO involved in all meetings?
4. How involved should the staff be?

Russ

From: Jack Billings
Sent: March 8 9:02 PM.
To: Russ Peterson
Subject: Re: Four very basic questions

Russ –

Sorry, it has been crazy the last few days, but now that I've got a few minutes, let me take your four questions in order.

1. How you set up the Planning and Resource Committee really depends on your organization's needs at a particular time. Are you emphasizing financial planning, long-range planning, or short-term planning? We have eight to ten members on our committee, but there is no perfect number. The key is flexibility. You should set up this committee according to what is necessary at a given time.

2. As we've talked about earlier, the Assessment Committee typically meets as a full group no more than four times a year. The full Planning and Resource Committee may meet more or less often, depending on the issues under consideration. Subcommittees, also known as ad hoc committees, meet as needed. They deal with a range of topics, such as personnel policies, OSHA requirements, and long-term space needs.

After making a report to the full committee, ad hoc committees disband.

3. Generally, the CEO attends all major committee meetings. He or she may or may not serve on subcommittees, depending on the information and guidance needed by the group.

4. Staff input is critical. Professional staffs make major contributions to board policy decisions through their involvement with the Planning and Resource Committee. (As CEO, I strive to foster an atmosphere in which my staff members feel free to express opinions in Planning and Resource meetings to board directors and to the administrative staff.) When confronted with a particularly difficult issue, an excellent means of communication is a board/staff workshop. Such a workshop brings staff and members of the Planning and Resource Committee together in a relaxed setting. Such workshops contribute greatly to our efforts to plan for programs. The interaction between board and staff enhances the quality of our decision making. There are also secondary benefits, as a workshop enhances professional communications between board and staff and engages board members in meaningful hands-on projects.

At times, the Corporate Model has been criticized for eliminating informal communication between the board and staff, since all operational communications are routed through the Executive Committee and CEO. As a practitioner and keen observer of the Model, I find this criticism unfair. Board members and staff members have ample opportunity to work together on task force projects that really have an impact on the organization. Such activity benefits the organization and isn't just social contact.

I just can't emphasize enough that board members and the top executive of a nonprofit must work together in an organized way to analyze the risks and opportunities that affect the organization. Too many boards have been content to analyze proposals endlessly (i.e., engage in analysis paralysis). Others, to avoid conflict, have tended to rubber-stamp proposals made by vocal or overly aggressive board members. Neither of these types of boards truly participates in the challenging act of establishing policy and direction for their nonprofit groups.

The times are certainly changing. Boards are being held much more personally accountable for their actions by the community and by legal statute. For example, if a volunteer board chair also assumes the CEO title, or becomes president/CEO, he or she may face increased exposure to liability for not meeting his or her duties of being very current on finances, compliance regulations, organizational limitations, etc.

Jack

P.S. Here's my summation of above:

THE CORPORATE MODEL PROMOTES ACCOUNTABILITY. IT REQUIRES THE BOARD AND THE CEO TO WORK TOGETHER TO PAINT THE BIG PICTURE FOR THE ORGANIZATION. IT THEN HOLDS THE CEO ACCOUNTABLE FOR IMPLEMENTING THAT VISION. THE PLANNING AND RESOURCE COMMITTEE PLAYS A MAJOR PART IN PAINTING THIS PICTURE BY HELPING THE ORGANIZATION AND THE CEO TO LOOK AHEAD TO THE FUTURE.

"I like how our new CEO moves! He manages all of our day-to-day operations so we concentrate on looking ahead."

6

THE MODEL AT WORK

*The Executive Committee
And Its Responsibilities*

From: Jack Billings
Sent: March 18 9:02 AM
To: Russ Peterson
Subject: Saturday night comment

Russ –

It's a quiet Sunday morning and I have to tell you about a conversation I had last night.

Ann and I were invited to a large dinner party where we were introduced to a number of guests. During the evening, one person happened to mention his involvement with a not-for-profit group in our community. Naturally, I was interested, particularly when I heard him note with some pride that he was a member of the organization's Executive Committee.

"We have a REAL BOARD," he told me. I asked him to explain what he meant, and he said that "a real board tells its executive director exactly WHAT TO DO." I made a mental note to avoid that nonprofit if I ever decide to look for a new job. Then I changed the subject. I didn't think it was appropriate to tell him what I really wanted to say: "You don't have a real board. What you have is a parent-child relationship."

When I got home last night, I thought of you and the concerns of your committee. What Yorkville has now, and what many nonprofits have clung to for so long, is a parent-child relationship. Like all such relationships, they come in many different forms. But Yorkville is discovering, albeit painfully, as are so many other nonprofits, that organizations outgrow the old structure and must find a new structure if they are to reach maturity.

You and I haven't yet talked about the work of the Executive Committee under the Corporate Model, and now seems an appropriate time to tackle the subject. I want us to approach the topic in a way that will help your committee really understand how things change under the Corporate Model. Let me suggest a method that I think should make it clear. The next time your restructuring committee meets, ask your colleagues to come up with a list of four or five issues that theoretically could come before the Executive Committee of a nonprofit group.

I'll then take those same issues and point out two different ways of responding to them. One will apply to Executive Committees with the traditional structure, wherein the board assumes a parental role. The other will apply to Executive Committees with the Corporate Model.

Jack

From: Russ Peterson
Sent: March 19 7:01 AM
To: Jack Billings
Subject: I like your offer

Jack,

Somehow you always seem to anticipate what my committee members need to know in order to truly understand the Model!

I didn't get around to checking e-mail yesterday, but last night I took a few minutes to jot down a handwritten list of the responsibilities of the Executive Committee. My list was based on notes I took when we talked over the Thanksgiving weekend. The list –

Under the Corporate Model, the Executive Committee:

- sets board meeting agendas
- acts for the full board between meetings, subject to later ratification by the full board
- receives all reports from the Assessment and the Planning and Resource Committees
- appoints all members of standing, ad hoc, and advisory committees

After making this list, I asked myself, "How is this Executive Committee different from any other?" I knew I would be hard pressed to answer that question. I was about ready to send you a quick e-mail this morning asking for your help when I saw an e-mail from you in my inbox.

I like your offer and I'm certain my Yorkville committee will too. Will get back to you after we meet later this month.

Russ

From: Russ Peterson
Sent: March 27 9:41 PM
To: Jack Billings
Subject: Five issues for you to address

Jack,

Had a committee meeting earlier today. After some discussion, we came up with five issues we'd like you to address about the Executive Committee:

1. Development of the annual budget
2. Budget deficits and cash-flow problems
3. A personnel issue, for example, the hiring of additional minority staff
4. Employee grievances
5. Interpersonal relationship between the board chair and the CEO

The committee is eager to explore this entire area. Is it possible for you to respond before my committee meets again on April 17? I know you're putting in a lot of time for us and I want you to know I appreciate all the effort.

My continuing thanks!

Russ

Executive Director

"I will be late – meeting with a group of directors. I wonder what office operations they will change this month."

From: Jack Billings
Sent: April 2 8:09 PM
To: Russ Peterson
Subject: Issue #1: budget development
Attachment: Exec Comm tackles budget.pdf

Russ –

I like your suggested topics. What I plan to do is address each issue in a separate memo. This will make it very easy to see the difference between the traditional board structure and the Corporate Model board. (I also know my schedule. If I try to do it all at once, it might not ever get done!) I'll forward each memo as I develop them. The first one is attached.

Jack

MEMORANDUM

TO: *Yorkville Committee on Restructuring*
FROM: *Jack Billings*
DATE: *April 1*
SUBJECT: *The Executive Committee and the Annual Budget*

Scenario: *The organization is developing its annual budget.*

THE TRADITIONAL BOARD

The Executive Committee oversees the entire budget process. Although it may delegate significant responsibility to the board finance committee members and to individual staff members, particularly to top staff, it remains in charge of the overall budget process. I've even observed situations where board finance committees get involved with deciding line items and budget details. Obviously, since the senior manager has ultimate financial responsibility for monitoring budget execution, he or she must be involved in its development. The level of detailed involvement will often depend on the level of his or her financial expertise and the level of trust the executive director has with the board.

By the time the budget is submitted to the full board for approval, the Executive Committee will probably have had countless budget meetings, sometimes lasting hours. Operational issues (such as individual salaries, maintenance schedules, and equipment purchases) may have been covered at length. In some organizations, the finance committee chairperson, not the executive director, presents the budget to the board. The day the budget is approved by the full board, most Executive Committee members feel they know every paper clip the nonprofit expects to purchase in the next twelve months!

This "top down" budget process has a long history. It dates from the time when board members of a nonprofit organization were viewed as having the expertise in fiscal and managerial issues. Professional staff members, on the other hand, were perceived as experts in delivering various types of service. In one children's service nonprofit in the early part of the twentieth century, the agency actually had two boards—a men's board to manage the finances and a women's board to assist the staff in caring for the children!

THE CORPORATE BOARD

One of the premises of the Corporate Model is that volunteers are part-timers and cannot and should not be expected to shoulder the financial and managerial burden that the budget process demands. (The considerable burdens of their own professions prevent most from acquiring the necessary knowledge relevant to the nonprofit organization.) In today's world, no reasonable business could operate effectively with such part-time expertise. A nonprofit should not be expected to operate this way either.

The Corporate Model structure recognizes that the president/CEO and the staff have the most thorough knowledge of the needs and resources of the organization. The Executive Committee expects the president/CEO to work with the staff to develop the budget within policy guidelines set by the board. The process tells the president/CEO that he or she is responsible for developing a budget and for presenting it to the Executive Committee for questions and discussion.

Subsequently, the president/CEO presents the budget to the full board. Because the board must ultimately approve the budget, directors must understand the budget process, ask tough questions, and be aware of the organization's financial needs and resources. But that does not mean the board usurps the president/CEO's responsibility to develop the budget. Instead, the board may appoint members to serve on a budget review committee (for example, the treasurer, a representative from the Assessment Committee, and a representative from the Planning and Resource Committee).

The Corporate Model recognizes that budgets are best developed from the bottom up under the direction of the CEO, the person who knows the most about the organization and has responsibility for executing policy directives. The president/CEO keeps the board informed of progress and, if necessary, educates the board on the budget process. He or she submits a complete and detailed document for approval and stands ready to answer questions and respond to board recommendations.

After the budget is approved, the Corporate Model board gives it back to the president/CEO and says, in effect, "Now it's your job to live within it."

From: Jack Billings
Sent: April 7 7:56 PM
To: Russ Peterson
Subject: Issue #2: deficits and cash flow
Attachment: Exec Comm—revenue issues.pdf

Russ –

FYI: Drafted this late last night. See attached.

Jack

MEMORANDUM

TO: *Yorkville Committee on Restructuring*
FROM: *Jack*
DATE: *April 6*
SUBJECT: *Deficits and Cash-Flow Problems and the Work of the Executive Committee*

Scenario: *For a variety of reasons, revenue has been much less than projected for the XYZ Nonprofit Association. If the current situation does not change, the organization will have a deficit of $18,000 for the entire year. The association also has an immediate cash-flow problem. Substantial payments due from two contracts have been delayed for three weeks. Without these payments, the association will be unable to meet its payroll two weeks from today.*

THE TRADITIONAL BOARD

The Executive Committee has been in session for hours. The board chairperson has delayed a trip in order to attend the special meeting. One can almost feel the tension in the room. Everyone has questions. "Why did this happen? What do we need to do to turn the situation around? Can we charge more for certain services? Should we revise the entire fee structure? Is it time to eliminate one or more programs? If we trim staff, what will the consequences be?"

After a lengthy, detailed discussion, the committee takes two steps. It authorizes the association to borrow $15,000 to cover the next payroll. The Executive Committee also asks the board finance committee to look at options for covering the entire expected deficit. The board chairperson is concerned about the amount of time the finance committee must spend in the next few weeks to investigate the situation and come up with a viable solution. However, she sees no alternative.

Before adjourning the meeting, the board chairperson turns to the two board members who are authorized to sign for a loan and asks if they can get together the next day. The chairperson is dismayed to learn that one of the two must be out of town on business for three days. New arrangements are made. Finally, late into the night, the Executive Committee adjourns. Every member is well aware that meetings like this one will probably occur again.

THE CORPORATE BOARD

The Executive Committee is in session in its regularly scheduled monthly meeting. The chairperson calls the meeting to order promptly at noon. One of the agenda items is a report from the Planning and Resource Committee. The president/CEO and the committee chairperson bring the Executive Committee up to date on the deficit situation. (Eight weeks previously, the president/CEO had informed the entire board that revenues were below projections and that a deficit was likely to occur if changes were not made. The chief problem, the president/CEO had said then, was that the association was facing new competition in one major service area. In addition, contract payments in another area were delayed. The CEO had suggested that the Planning and Resource Committee meet with him and key staff members to see what could be done.)

The Planning and Resource Committee chairperson reports that the recent review session was productive. As a result of that meeting, the president/CEO had:

- put a four-month freeze on hiring
- delayed the opening of a new satellite office
- moved to make its key service area more physically attractive
- conducted additional staff in-service training to smooth out some newly identified problems that were adversely affecting cash flow
- taken steps to move more quickly in making planned program changes discussed four months ago by the president/CEO and members of the Planning and Resource Committee

The president/CEO, in his report, tells the Executive Committee that initial results from these changes are encouraging. The association should be able to avoid the projected deficit. "One thing that really helps," he says, "is that the association is able to move quickly when we see a problem ahead of us."

The president/CEO also notes that he borrowed $15,000 to cover the anticipated cash-flow problem caused by the unexpected delay in the contract payments. (The president has the authority to borrow up to $75,000 for short-term cash-flow problems.)

Following other reports, the chairperson adjourns the meeting. The Executive Committee session ends at 1:40 p.m., just a little later than usual.

Two weeks later, the entire situation was reported to the full board in detail for discussion, review, and ratification. However, during this two-week period several knowledgeable board members were informally apprised of the situation by the president/CEO. This avoided the surprise element no board should tolerate.

From: Jack Billings
Sent: April 9 7:31 AM
To: Russ Peterson
Subject: Issue #3: human resource issues
Attachment: Exec Comm _personnel issues.pdf

Russ –

FYI: Memo on your #3 issue is attached. Finished it last night and just reread!

Jack

TO: *Yorkville Committee on Restructuring*
FROM: *Jack*
DATE: *April 8*
SUBJECT: *The Executive Committee and Human Resource Issues*

MEMORANDUM

Scenario: *The nonprofit agency ABC has been criticized for not having enough minority staff members. Because ABC, a large, well-known organization, primarily serves urban residents in a major U.S. city, board members are concerned about the criticism.*

THE TRADITIONAL BOARD

The Executive Committee meets in a regular session. Spread out before each member are half a dozen copies of articles criticizing the organization for having too few minority staff members. The articles have appeared in the local newspaper and on blogs in the past week. Social networking media have carried the message further.

Emotions run high at the meeting. Many board members feel the organization has been treated too harshly both in print and online. The hiring and training of minority staff members has been an agenda topic at least three different times in the past six months. (Actually, the topic had first been raised eighteen months ago in the Personnel Committee, which had not fully considered the question because it had been tied up for months settling a grievance related to health benefits for several retirees.)

Two times in the past eight months, the Executive Committee had discussed the minority staff issue but had run out of time and tabled it for later consideration. During a third discussion initiated by a member at a full board meeting, the board had been unable to agree on a solution. Instead, since the Personnel Committee agenda was full, a special ad hoc committee had been formed. The ad hoc committee was due to report back in another month.

Executive Committee members argue that the existence of that special committee should have been pointed out in the newspaper articles. They spend most of the remainder of the meeting discussing how to counteract the negative publicity the organization has received and asking the executive director his views about the most effective way to use social media to the organization's advantage. Several members maintain that if the organization had a board member with public relations experience, this situation would never have occurred.

THE CORPORATE BOARD

The Executive Committee did not read about the lack of minority staff in newspaper articles, on blogs, online posts, in text messages, or in other places. The criticism was contained in a report presented at the last meeting by the board's Assessment Committee. The report pointed out that the CEO should have taken action that was more decisive in this area.

At today's meeting, Executive Committee members agree that the organization must take steps to hire and train more minority staff. The president/CEO agrees that this issue needs to be a higher priority on his operational agenda. He says he will discuss the topic again in four weeks. He also will update the personnel plan developed two years earlier. Evidently, that plan is not achieving its objectives.

From: Jack Billings
Sent: April 11 7:59 AM.
To: Russ Peterson
Subject: Issue #4: employee grievances
Attachment: Exec Comm _grievances.pdf

Russ –

See my answers to your #4. Up early this morning—inspired to write on this issue!

Now dashing to get to 8:45 meeting!

Jack

MEMORANDUM

TO: *Yorkville Committee on*
            Restructuring
FROM: *Jack*
DATE: *April 11*
SUBJECT: *Employee Grievances and the*
            Executive Committee

Scenario – A: *A high-level staff member calls the board chair at home at night to complain that he had not received a raise. The chairperson has worked with this staff member many times over the years and respects his work.*

Scenario – B: *A member of the Executive Committee receives a call from another staff member who complains he received a negative evaluation by his supervisor. The staff member says the evaluation was unfair and asks the board member to intervene on his behalf.*

THE TRADITIONAL BOARD

Scenario – A: The board chairperson calls the executive director and tells him that in order to be "fair" to a highly competent staff member, the matter should be brought to the Executive Committee. The chairperson presents the case at the next Executive Committee meeting. For twenty minutes, committee members discuss the work of the employee in question. They also question the executive director about the situation. Committee members ask the executive director to leave the room while they consider the matter. Finally, they agree to a pay increase of $200 a month. The raise is made retroactive to the previous month.

Scenario – B: After receiving the staff member's call, the board member calls the organization's executive director and asks her for more details. After listening to her report, the board member says he agrees with the evaluation of the staff member. He tells the executive director he will report their conversation to the staff member who called.

THE CORPORATE BOARD

Scenario – A: The board chairperson tells the high-level staff member to take his request for a raise directly to the president/CEO. The chairperson is well aware that by stepping in to solve the problem he would undermine the authority of the president/CEO.

Scenario – B: The Executive Committee member tells the staff member to discuss the negative evaluation with his supervisor again. If they cannot agree, he should discuss the situation with the president/CEO (the supervisor's immediate boss). Later the president/CEO calls to say, "I appreciate the way you handled this matter. We were able to work out the problem in a face-to-face meeting."

From: Jack Billings
Sent: April 13 7:44 AM
To: Russ Peterson
Subject: Issue #5: interpersonal
               relationships
Attachment: Exec Comm relationship chair-
               CEO.pdf

Russ –

FYI: Memo on your last issue (#5) is attached. Will review all memos and see if I left anything out. Be back to you on that within days.

Jack

MEMORANDUM

TO: *Yorkville Committee on Restructuring*
FROM: *Jack*
DATE: *April 13*
SUBJECT: *Interpersonal relationships between board chairperson and the CEO*

Scenario: *Newly elected board chair is being briefed on responsibilities by outgoing board chairperson. At the moment, the outgoing chairperson is discussing his relationship with the CEO and the nonprofit's staff*

THE TRADITIONAL BOARD

"People are always telling me that they see my car parked outside the agency an awful lot. It's true that sometimes I feel as though I'm 'in residence' here. I spend a lot of time in meetings with the CEO, and though that takes a great deal of the CEO's time, I believe my input has been very helpful for the organization. A lot of staff feel comfortable talking with me about various issues and problems. I guess you could say I've developed my own informal communication channels with staff members. Many of them view me as the authority—maybe even a parent figure—here. I've felt I've been able to contribute a lot working this way. The first thing I recommend you do when you take over this position is get yourself a regular parking space just outside the front door."

THE CORPORATE BOARD

"Our CEO is the professional in this organization. She's an excellent manager with expertise in the field and that's why we hired her for the top job. My job, as board chair, has not been to stand by her side at all times, debating her every move, and discussing problems with staff. I've viewed my role as being a supporter and board leader. That means I've appeared here as needed and made myself available as an adviser to the CEO and to others designated by her.

"At the same time, I recognized early on that I had as much of a responsibility as the CEO to build the communication channel between us. We met and talked about how best to work together. As a result, both of us have been very willing to call on our cell phones and talk about key issues, or dash off an e-mail to one another when needed. We've developed great professional respect for one another and are willing to listen even when we have a difference of opinion on a subject. I have no doubt you too can develop this same kind of excellent working relationship.

"As chair, I've also been responsible for what I call 'institutional memory'—in other words, the history of this organization—and for keeping the board on track in terms of policy issues and for making certain that policy proposals that come before the board are acted upon and implemented when adopted. It's been my job, and now will be your job, to maintain the Corporate Model and to ensure new board members are trained in how it works. I can't overemphasize how critical this training is. If it isn't undertaken on a regular basis, new board members can become confused about their roles and responsibilities. New board members, out of a sense of 'gaining comfort,' may want to return to the traditional governance models that are more costly and less efficient.

"Being board chair carries a lot of responsibility, but that doesn't mean you have to end up practically living here."

From: Jack Billings
Sent: April 15 8:42 PM
To: Russ Peterson
Subject: Quick final thoughts

Russ –

Have just a few last thoughts about the Executive Committee under the Corporate Model.

Do remember that all reports and actions from standing committees go through the Executive Committee before going to the full board. All ad hoc committee reports go through both the Planning and Resource and Executive Committees before they are submitted to the board. This system promotes information flow and leads to effective and efficient meetings, which, in turn, do not waste your board members' valuable time. Through this process most directors on boards that have up to twenty-five members, become familiar with what reports are moving forward long before they need to be discussed at board meetings.

I hope that my scenarios help you understand why I favor giving the CEO the right to vote. It is a sign of authority. Since the CEO represents the staff, it also gives the staff a voice on the board, albeit indirectly.

The Corporate Model allows for outside advisory committees that are appointed by the Executive Committee. Advisory committee representatives can attend board meetings, except when the board goes into executive session. Outside advisory committees should work closely with a nonprofit's staff to ensure that the information they provide will improve operations.

Jack

P.S. THINK OF THE EXECUTIVE COMMITTEE AS AN EXPEDITING GROUP. BY DOING ITS WORK WELL, IT ALLOWS THE FULL BOARD TO CONCENTRATE ON IMPORTANT POLICY ISSUES.

BTW: WE'VE NOW COVERED THE MODEL'S STRUCTURE AND THE ASSESSMENT, PLANNING AND RESOURCE, AND EXECUTIVE COMMITTEES—IN OTHER WORDS, ALL THE PARTS OF THE CORPORATE MODEL.

7

THE MODEL CREATES
A NEW CULTURE

Trust Is the Critical Factor

From: Russ Peterson
Sent: April 18 7:31 AM
To: Jack Billings
Subject: Culture change & board engagement

Jack,

After last night's meeting, my Yorkville committee is close to recommending that we adopt the
Corporate Model. However, two areas of concern
remain.

We think that we need to know more about the
new culture created by the Corporate Model. We
also need more information about how to keep
board members truly involved without the ego
satisfaction that often comes from dealing with
operational issues.

Your assistance has been invaluable. Can you
help us with these two final areas?

Russ

From: Jack Billings
Sent: April 20 5:36 PM
To: Russ Peterson
Subject: Talking culture & involvement

Russ –

Waited a couple days to respond so I could confirm my schedule and tell you your timing is terrific!

I'm going to be in Yorkville on business for two days in mid-May. I have meetings with my counterpart in Yorkville on Thursday and Friday, May 15 and 16, and will be tied up both days and Thursday evening. If you don't mind having a houseguest Friday night, I'd be willing to meet with your committee Friday evening and Saturday morning. We could devote the first session to "culture" and the second to "involvement."

Would your committee members be willing to give up part of their weekend on such short notice? The alternative, of course, would be for the two of us to talk.

Jack

P.S. How about dinner with you two at that great restaurant we enjoyed so much last time Ann and I were in town? I should be free by 4:30 that Friday.

From: Russ Peterson
Sent: April 27 12:10 PM
To: Jack Billings
Subject: Re: Talking culture & involvement

Jack,

We're set for your visit. Only one committee member can't make it Friday evening. Saturday morning looks clear for everyone in the restructuring group.

I'll treat you to dinner before the Friday night session.

Saturday we'll start at 7:30 a.m. I promise to have coffee and bagels on hand.

Both sessions will be at my house. If the weather is good, we should be able to get in at least nine holes of golf after Saturday's meeting ends!

Russ

BTW: Jack, I plan to video both sessions. For a small fee (we'll see!), my son said he would transcribe and edit the tapes, so I'll have a record of the dialogue. I'll send you copies.

From: Russ Peterson
Sent: May 25 12:34 PM
To: Jack Billings
Subject: Transcription—Friday night
Attachment: Model creates new culture.pdf

Jack,

The edited transcript of our Friday discussion is attached.

Note that unless otherwise indicated, you are the person speaking.

Comments and questions by other speakers are in italics.

I'll send you the edited transcript for the Saturday morning session when it is complete.

Russ

First Discussion
"The Model Creates a New Culture"

We've been corresponding—through Russ—for so many months I really feel that I know all of you. I've been looking forward to getting together tonight. I really enjoy talking about the Corporate Model and appreciate having a forum!

When you talk about the new kind of culture that must exist for a Corporate Model board, you're talking about something intangible, but absolutely key, to a change like the one you are contemplating.

Some months ago, a magazine article caught my attention because I thought the author made his points rather succinctly about how to think about effective board culture. His comments were voiced in questions. Are discussions on the board relevant, rigorous, and probing? Do just a few directors dominate because they commandeer the discussion? Are there factions on the board? Is board chemistry volatile or collaborative? Do superficial statements go unchallenged? Is the board equipped to deal with the potential life-threatening issues for the organization?

Since I'm a storyteller at heart, let me tell several that will help me bring the concept of new culture to life, and in the process help you add context to the questions asked by that magazine writer. After that, feel free to ask me any and everything you might want to know about how the Model creates a new culture.

My first story is about my friend Sam, who told me over lunch recently about his problems as a member of the board of a nonprofit organization. Sam is a busy guy who agreed to join this board because

he really believes in what the organization is doing. Yet, Sam is finding the board job more time-
consuming and frustrating than he ever imagined.

Sam's board has devoted a major part of the past
three months to hiring a new vice president. The
position has been discussed by the board's personnel and executive committees, and by the
full board. Sam is on the personnel committee,
which spent three long sessions just discussing
the wording in the job description.

"Everyone knows we need to fill that position
soon, but the process seems to be taking forever,"
Sam told me. He was particularly upset that the
top candidate for the job got tired of waiting and
decided to withdraw his application.

Sam was amazed when I told him I'd hired a
new vice president just last month and my board
wasn't involved at all. I said we had selected a
terrific person and made the changeover in record time. Within minutes, we discovered that
my new VP was the very person who had given
up on Sam's organization!

The point to remember here is that presidents/
CEOs under the Corporate Model have much more
responsibility for their organizations than do executive directors in traditional nonprofit groups.

They can move faster and be more creative. They can hire and fire without endless committee discussions. They are responsible for all personnel changes below their level. The Model, in fact, is specifically designed to delegate a high level of authority to management. Board culture is extremely important because board members must be at a point where they feel comfortable with this level of delegation, and the senior manager must embrace—with enthusiasm—the increased responsibility.

Here's an analogy I like. Think of your organization as a ship. The board of directors determines the ship's destination. The president/CEO has command of who is staffing the ship and is responsible for getting the ship to its destination in the most efficient and effective manner.

Obviously, the CEO should routinely keep the board informed about personnel changes at a high level. However, the Corporate Model board generally has little interest in changes relating to operational staffing. The one outstanding exception may be when the CEO wants to hire an "unusual staff member," that is, someone who is not filling a traditional staff position. Although the CEO still has the responsibility for hiring, he or she should review the need for the position with the board. The board should reverse the CEO's decision only if the long-term prospects for the position and the costs involved do not fall within the approved budget strategy.

By the way, for information purposes, I take a few minutes each quarter to highlight staff changes and activities for my own board.

The point of my first story is that with the Corporate Model directors respect the CEO's ability to run the organization. Unfortunately, it is not uncommon to have one or two trustees who love to micromanage management and staff. When that situation occurs, and that type of interference can become intolerable, the board chair must intervene.

My second story concerns a nonprofit organization that operates under the Corporate Model. Recently, the president/ CEO discovered, quite by accident, that a former staff member in the personnel office has copies of some confidential payroll spreadsheets.

When the CEO asked the former employee for the copies, the individual refused to give them to her. The former staff member feels that he has a right to the copies because they relate to the work he performed for the organization.

Well, the top execs of many nonprofits would run immediately to the board for help. However, this

CEO recognizes that she's paid to be a problem solver. She wants the board to know about the situation but also is concerned about protecting the organization, the board, and its individual members from any legal liability that may result from the situation. This CEO made an appointment to see a lawyer and invited the board chairperson to accompany her. With the guidance of the lawyer, the CEO verbally reported the situation to the board along with the lawyer's recommended actions.

The important thing is not how this situation was ultimately resolved, but how the chief executive handled it. A traditional board would have dropped the problem like a "hot potato" into the hands of board members. On the Corporate Model board, the president/CEO plays quarterback. As you know, that's a significant difference.

My third and final story is about a nonprofit organization I'm sure will sound familiar to you. There are countless organizations just like it throughout the country. This particular nonprofit is large, and it operates a significant number of programs. Recently a new director was hired to run these programs. The board selected the person for the job and determined her salary with only modest attention to the advice of its executive director. Not surprisingly, the new program director does not have much respect for her boss.

In fact, when she has a problem with a program she takes it directly to the board.

Unusual? It happens more often than you realize. However, it never happens on a Corporate Model board that functions as it should. In reality, you can't have a Corporate Model board unless you have a chief executive officer who is really in charge of operations. As I've mentioned several times before, a board of directors that adopts the Model places a great deal of responsibility and authority in the hands of its president/CEO. The board must be sure that the individual it selects for the job not only can handle the position but also will be comfortable in it. Once that decision is made, board members must place their faith and trust in their new executive.

Trust is an essential ingredient here. If board members do not trust and respect their CEO, one of two things will happen. Either the Model will fail or the CEO will leave. It's particularly important that the board chair, other directors, and the CEO personally trust each other. They must view the CEO as a competent executive, not as an expert in direct service who needs help with management activities. Whether the CEO came up via the direct service route is unimportant. As CEO, his or her first job is to manage. In return, the members of a Corporate Board must stand back and let him or her do the job.

Now, before we open this up to questions, I just want to make a few brief points about the relationship between a board chair and the CEO and vice versa.

First, in order to maintain trust between the chair and CEO, the chair must be certain that the evaluation of the organization and the personal evaluation of the CEO are inclusive, i.e., cover a balance of the most relevant outcomes. Otherwise, the evaluation outcomes have the potential to damage the trust relationship that's necessary to drive organizational growth. If the evaluation has a negative tone to it, and the CEO is being given time to improve performance, the chair needs to take steps to reduce unproductive tensions until the CEO's performance improves—or, alternatively, there's a decision made that it is time to change CEOs.

Second, what if you have a situation where the chemistry between the board chair and the CEO is problematic? Let's say the CEO is politically liberal and the chair is very conservative. In cases like these, boards often have trouble maintaining civil discourse at meetings. I've not faced that problem, but I have colleagues who have. On the Corporate Model board, the CEO needs to be strong enough to have a frank talk with his or her board chair to get the situation back on track. What you are looking for is "balance."

Third, an essential ingredient in board culture is the CEO's ability to be flexible. He or she needs to accommodate to a new boss every year or two. If you have a Corporate Model board you simply can't have a complacent CEO. He or she needs to be alert, to recognize when the board—often initiated by the chair—wants to move in a new direction.

Now let's open this up for questions. I suspect you have some.

Jack, how do you know when you've achieved this new kind of culture?

As I mentioned, board culture is really about having chemistry that works. Is there transparency, and by that I mean openness? It's an intangible, but it is critical. Is there a spirit of inquiry? That means, for example, that a trustee can disagree with another trustee or with the CEO without actually being hostile or being viewed as hostile for having an opposing opinion. Do you have a few really insightful board members who spark real dialogue? I'm talking about people who can literally smell "opportunity" or "problem" or "roadblock." Do you have creativity—from the CEO and from board members?

And while I'm on the subject of creativity let me mention one thing in passing. One of the biggest complaints from directors is that too many CEOs absolutely depend on PowerPoint presentations to make their case. Directors aren't upset such presentations are utilized by CEOs because they can be helpful. Directors hate them when they are far too long, the slides are overwhelmingly dense, or they touch on issues tangential to the case being made, or frankly are being used to stifle real dialogue. (Some business organizations limit PowerPoint presentations to a maximum of ten slides, even for complex venture capital or budget requests.)

Next, are you tapping the creativity on your board? Don't let board culture mold a new director to an expected narrow framework. In other words, don't have a strong financial manager become involved with the details of the organization's budget. Instead, use his or her expertise to help develop an intelligent overall financial strategy, which can make an impact on the organization's future. In fact, when we have orientation sessions for our new board directors, I attend the orientation sessions and point out where they might creatively apply their expertise.

Finally, getting back to the notion of being insightful—are there board members who know whether the board is dealing with symptoms or causes? Here's an example of what I mean.

Do they know cash flow is a problem for your organization or do they know why cash flow is a problem? Do they know that your top competitor has introduced something new or do they know why that something new is causing negative ripples in your own organization?

Remember too, in today's complex world, your board should not be primarily focused on outcomes (e.g., success of specific programs) but concerned more about assessing the "impacts" of those outcomes. Here's an example of what I mean. Heard it at a presentation by Geoffrey Canada. Lots of people have heard about the Harlem Children's Zone he initiated. What is his real goal? He absolutely wants poor urban students to show that they can and do succeed, but that's not the impact he seeks. His real goal is to seed the Harlem community with individuals who lived there while they were growing up and return to Harlem after they graduate from college. Impact is much harder than outcome to measure because it is about something that is far more ambitious.

But that's why we're talking about the Corporate Model—because it is about being effective.

Jack, can you give us a couple of other real-life examples of how this new culture works? Talk about some things that are more everyday in nature than the case of the employee with the confidential documents.

Two examples come to mind immediately.

As you probably guessed, I've served on a number of nonprofit boards over the years. The volunteer president of one of these organizations, a nonprofit association with a traditional structure, always made it a practice to notify the full-time executive director when he planned to take a vacation. In essence, the volunteer president was asking, "Is this an appropriate time for me to be gone? Can you handle things while I'm away?" In some cases, the executive director even delayed making his own travel plans until the two of them had conferred.

This kind of situation wouldn't exist with the Corporate Model. It would be assumed that the CEO is in control of the organization. Out of courtesy, the chairperson might inform the CEO when he or she would be out of town. Should the CEO decide to be out of town at the same time, he or she must arrange for appropriate staff backup. As a courtesy, the CEO should inform the chairperson about travel plans. Let me note here, however, that only once in four years has it been necessary for my chairperson and me to be in contact while one of us was out of town.

My other everyday example of the culture at work is from my own organization. Two years ago, we had a new employee who wanted to see his methods of improving staff morale put to work. This individual sent an e-mail to each board member, saying that he had noticed that staff morale was poor. He also detailed his suggestions for improving the situation. Because everyone received the e-mail, the issue was raised at the next Executive Committee session. Two members of the committee opened the discussion by saying, "This is an issue for management, not the board." I was asked to address the situation and to provide information about it. That kind of comment wouldn't have been made on a more traditional board. The board probably would have wanted to get in and personally investigate.

But let me add a note of caution here. Sometimes an individual with just that type of concern might be alerting the board to a growing, unrecognized problem. Some larger boards may want to establish a "hot line" system, as mandated by Sarbanes-Oxley for public corporations, to make certain they are not overlooking a problem. Nonprofit board members walk a fine line in these situations.

Jack, I've been on the Yorkville board for a long time now. Until recently, it wasn't unusual for us to meet every couple of months without the executive director. Would that ever happen on a Corporate Model board?

No. The CEO's involvement is central to the success of the Corporate Model. Here's where that issue of trust comes into play. For the full board to meet without its top executive really says, "We can't trust you to run this place." Under normal conditions, the only time the board or any important committee should exclude the CEO is when the Assessment Committee meets with the outside auditors to review the yearly audit and management letter. Let me note, however, that since Sarbanes-Oxley has suggested independent directors on for-profit boards meet in executive sessions without inside directors (management), I have a feeling there are more executive sessions being scheduled on nonprofit boards.

That shouldn't be happening on nonprofit boards with the Corporate Model. If there's a problem with the CEO on a Corporate Model board, it'll be obvious in board assessment reports. If the CEO is going to be fired, he or she will know it. Termination won't come as a surprise to anyone. On the other hand, in traditionally structured nonprofits, I've seen situations where executives have been given glowing evaluations by their board and then fired six or eight months later.

Do you think an exec who has worked only under a more traditional structure can make the transition to the Model?

Absolutely—as long as that individual understands his or her new role and is comfortable in it. Let's talk specifically for a moment. I've known Joyce Thomas, your executive director, for some time now. She has excellent administrative skills. She and I have even had some conversations about the Corporate Model. I suspect she'd welcome the change.

On the other hand, I've had many executive directors tell me there's no way they would want the kind of responsibility I have, especially given the technology-driven environment and the fundraising needs that we have today. This type of person is not a candidate for CEO of an organization with the Corporate Model.

The Model allows the CEO a measure of fiscal latitude. Just how much latitude should the CEO have?

Once the board approves the operating budget for the year, it monitors the organization's financial status monthly and annually. The CEO reports monthly expenditures and income by major areas. At each regular monthly meeting, the CEO also informs the board about any budget developments and exceptions. A thorough assessment of how the organization is doing financially is conducted annually by the Assessment Committee, including the review of the yearly audit by the outside auditing firm.

My board's trust is shown most graphically by the fact that I can borrow, on my own, up to $100,000 on a short-term basis when we have a cash-flow problem.

OK. We have an executive director who could make the switch but I wonder about our board chairperson. He is used to having an active program committee study every issue from every angle. He wants to know about every nickel the organization spends.

It's simple. If your chairperson can't change his or her style, you need a new one—someone who's comfortable with new ways of doing things. For example, you won't need countless board program committee meetings—that's why you have staff.

I can understand how fiscal latitude gives the CEO the freedom she or he needs to spend money on behalf of the organization. What I don't understand is who in the organization is responsible for fund-raising? Isn't that an area in which the

CEO should follow the board?

When it comes to fund-raising, and this is a significant area we haven't really covered before, the board and the CEO have mutual responsibility. As president/CEO in an organization using the Corporate Model, I'm really the advance guard when it comes to fund-raising. First and foremost, I have to be alert to all the places where I can raise funds on my own. This involves everything from developing grant requests to understanding where public funds can be obtained to knowing about national and local sources that might support my organization's goals. Obviously, I don't do all this alone. My staff is there to assist me.

My next responsibility is to work closely with directors on the board who have development backgrounds, skills, contacts, and the interest to expand the effort to attract resources from a wider range of organizations and individuals. This is a usually a small group. Although some directors may be affluent and may make substantial contributions to the organization themselves, they may hesitate to become involved in the organization's development effort.

Let me give you an example of how this works with my board.

A year ago, my staff and I identified a need in our community that we felt our organization was well equipped to meet. After we designed a program that would assist the specific population in question, I took our proposal to the board. I explained the reason for proposing the program, and board members concurred with me that we should move ahead. We discussed fund-raising objectives outlined in the program proposal, and over the next few weeks I asked several board directors to assist me in opening doors or making calls. At times, board members made their own calls. At other times, we made joint calls. We evaluated each situation to determine the best approach.

Let me sum all this up with a simple analogy. When it comes to raising funds, consider the president/CEO the forward scout looking for a potential source of funds. The board—the cavalry—is called in to support that effort and broaden the base of support. In other words, the scout gives the signal, but the cavalry is needed to take the objective.

Do you ever make use of board directors in your scouting party?

Yes, I do. If you are lucky enough to have a forward-looking board member with well-developed fund-raising skills, you'll probably quickly discover, as we have, that the individual can give you new insights into achieving your goals. For example, I have a terrific board director who helped lead us into an entirely new field of service and opened many donors' doors. All of this resulted from the experiences and information she gained on another board in another city.

Should all board members be required to be involved with fund-raising?

As I indicated, the simple answer is "no"—just those who have done it before or are willing, with some coaching, to try it. However, you want to maximize your board members' contacts. That may involve teaming someone who does not usually get involved in fund-raising with an experienced hand if the inexperienced person knows a potential donor.

If you adopt the Corporate Model, your CEO will need to be an assertive leader when it comes to fund-raising, but all of you, as board members, must play an active supporting role. Let me emphasize here that a nonprofit board does not abdicate its fund-raising responsibilities just because it hires a strong CEO.

And, believe me, neither my CEO colleagues nor I should ever assume we can abdicate our fund-raising responsibilities because we have board members! Thanks to the Internet, I recently came across a media story highlighting survey findings from a nonprofit governance index, published by the well-known Board Source organization. In that survey, published in 2010, nonprofit chief executives gave their boards D+ grades in fund-raising and rated them just a C+ overall. Both nonprofit chief executives and board members agreed that fund-raising was the area in which their boards most needed to improve. Next came strategic planning, and having an increased focus on strategic priorities—over operational issues—was third. For me, that story was another example of why I like the Corporate Model approach.

Unless you have other questions about fund-raising, I have just one further point I want to be sure to make tonight. Everyone on your board should be making an annual contribution. Certainly, the amount depends on each individual director's personal situation, but even a token amount is significant. When you're developing proposals, especially grant proposals for foundations or corporations, funders want to know whether all members of a board are behind the organization.

I like the fact that the Model makes the job of the top executive more entrepreneurial. However,

because the CEO has so much authority and be-
cause the board places so much trust in the indi-
vidual, isn't it easy for the CEO to overstep his or
her boundaries?

It happens. When it does, it's the board's job to
inform the CEO that he or she has taken on too
much authority. I was guilty of that myself recently. I signed a long-term contract that should
have gone first to the board. I typically sign routine contracts on my own, but the longevity of this
one meant it should have had board approval first,
even though the dollars involved with the contract
were very small. I recognized my error when it
was pointed out by my board chairperson, who
asked for formal board ratification of the contract.
None of us does our job perfectly. But a CEO has
to recognize who is the ultimate authority. In a
nonprofit organization, it's the board of directors.

Doesn't the Model require more trust between
board and CEO than you would find in the for-
profit world?

It does. I don't believe you need as much trust in
the for-profit world because the bottom line can
give you a reasonably clear (not exact) indication
of how the CEO is performing. In the nonprofit world, you have no solid bottom line, except
the one that says income must match expenses.

Board directors must trust in the ability of the person they have selected to do the job. They must hold that person accountable for doing the job. In my experience, a tipping point at which trust can come apart is related to performance evaluation. Since there is no comprehensive performance bottom line for many nonprofit organizations, and the cost of obtaining solid quantitative performance metrics is so high, most nonprofits have to rely on imperfect metrics.

Jack, we have to wrap this up for tonight if we're going to get together early tomorrow. You've convinced me of just how important this new environment, this new culture, is to the Model.

One brief final comment! It seems that trust under the Model is like trust in a marriage. You don't want to marry a person you don't trust. You also don't change to the Corporate Model unless you have, or can hire, a president/CEO in whom you can place a reasonable amount of trust.

"It used to take three board people to do what our CEO now does easily on her own"

THE MODEL AND COMMITMENT

Board Members Must Be Involved

From: Russ Peterson
Sent: May 29 7:12 PM
To: Jack Billings
Subject: Transcription—Saturday session
Attachment: Model creates new culture2.pdf

Jack,

Here's the edited transcript from our Saturday session. I've followed the same format that I used in the transcript of the Friday night session. Italics are used to identify other speakers.

Russ

P.S. The restructuring committee is meeting early in June to begin drafting our report to the Yorkville board. Will keep you posted on developments.

Second Discussion
"Board Members Must Be Involved"

Good morning! We're here to talk about "involvement." And I'm not at all surprised that you want me to address this topic. Whenever I talk about the Corporate Model to any group, I'm invariably asked one question: "If a board isn't involved in the day-to-day concerns of an organization and meets less frequently, won't directors soon lose interest in the organization?"

My answer is always the same. "No they won't, not if you keep them informed and they have specific, worthwhile tasks to accomplish for your not-for-profit group." People volunteer as board members of nonprofit groups for all sorts of reasons. Some have benefited, firsthand, from services provided by the nonprofit. Some have skills they want to utilize. Others volunteer because they want to expand their personal or professional contacts. Most care deeply about what the organization is seeking to achieve. One could go on and on. It's the job of the chairperson and the CEO to understand why a person has volunteered and to match that person's skills and interests to the needs of the nonprofit.

Let's talk specifically about Yorkville for a moment. We'll assume your board has adopted the Corporate Model. President/CEO Joyce Thomas and her staff hypothetically are now deciding whether to buy new equipment, increase insurance coverage, fire the custodian, hire a new program director, choose new furniture for the reception area, revise budget forms, revamp the accounting department, and so forth. In the past, board members had a big part in those activities. Now you and your fellow Yorkville directors are free to grapple with the bigger issues. For example:

- What kind of organization is Yorkville going to be in the future? What are the threats and opportunities in the field?
- Should it provide all of the services it now provides?
- Should it provide any new services?
- What does the financial future look like?
- What's the impact of rising costs?
- Is there a need for more emphasis on fund-raising?
- How would staff cutbacks affect services?

When they tackle these kinds of questions, board members truly invest themselves in the organization. Let me explain by painting a picture of what three Yorkville directors might, theoretically, end up doing on your Corporate Model board.

Director A is particularly interested in finding out whether programs that have been in existence for some time are still viable or whether they should be revamped or discontinued in light of some new communications technologies that are being developed. When the chairperson asks Director A if she will serve on the Assessment Committee, she willingly agrees.

Director A's first assignment is to work with two other committee members to evaluate Yorkville's information technology capabilities. Their task is to talk with the agency's IT specialists and other staff and then to make recommendations about the future impact of IT on the organization's programs. Their findings and recommendations will be communicated to the full Assessment Committee and then to the Executive Committee and the full board.

At the same time, Director B, who has agreed to serve on the Planning and Resource Committee, volunteers for a joint board/staff ad hoc subcommittee assigned to evaluate the feasibility of starting a new pilot program. A community group has approached Yorkville and asked that it consider providing certain limited off-site services for the elderly.

Director B will head the five-member group charged with determining whether this kind of program is appropriate for Yorkville. The subcommittee must determine whether such a service fits within the organization's spectrum of services, whether Yorkville is capable of entering into such a venture, and whether the community would view Yorkville as an adequate service provider. The subcommittee expects to make a report to the full Planning and Resource Committee within two months.

Director C, a local accountant, is particularly interested in the financial health of the organization.

He agrees to serve on the subcommittee assigned to investigate options for improving Yorkville's financial position. One of those options involves hiring a part-time development specialist for the organization. Director C anticipates his group's report will be in the hands of the full board within the next twelve weeks.

Note that all three of these directors work with small groups on specific tasks. They have clear goals to achieve. When they complete their tasks, all three directors will feel that their talents have been utilized in important ways to benefit Yorkville.

Members of Corporate Model boards will stay interested and involved in their nonprofit organizations if they are convinced that their activities have a purpose and serve the organization. I know this from personal experience. And a side note here. Being pertinent and time-limited is especially applicable for younger individuals building a career not only because they often lead busy lives but also because this age group is now used to immediate gratification and to projects that last no longer than the equivalent of a semester.

Finally, my own board members repeatedly say they like the way the board works. Assignments are interesting and well organized. They feel useful here. That's what you'd want for Yorkville.

I'm sure you have questions. Why don't I answer them now?

What you're saying about board members' involvement could apply to any nonprofit board operating under the Corporate Model, couldn't it?

Certainly. Only the details would change. For example, you can investigate the pros and cons of starting a new pilot program at Yorkville or you can investigate expanding program offerings at a nonprofit trade association.

Under the Model, the CEO and staff make all the operational decisions. Only rarely will board members be invited by the CEO to participate. Yet, doesn't the board still need to know what's going on in operations?

No doubt about it. The name of the game for the CEO is to communicate the important information to board members and to keep them informed of significant developments. Still, there's no need to clutter regular board meetings by reporting endless details about operations. Probably the most effective way of keeping board members aware of what is going on within the organization is to have staff frequently make short presentations at board meetings.

Another technique is to use a *consent agenda*. With a consent agenda, routine and previously agreed upon items are organized together in the pre-meeting agenda and then, hopefully, approved as a group. If one or more board members question a specific item in the group, it is placed on the agenda for the next board meeting. Routine items that need to be brought before the board can be placed on this agenda, instead of a having a separate discussion for each one.

However, I can't emphasize how important it is to meet with board members informally as well as formally. My secretary keeps a log of informal contacts, and if I don't have an informal contact with each board member every three months, she organizes a breakfast or lunch meeting so we can talk informally. Occasionally, I meet with two directors at the same time. Naturally, I meet with the board chair more often.

At these meetings I provide an update, discuss current challenges, and cover the more "entrepreneurial or even wild" ideas I have. Some of the meetings can happen quite informally, before or after a committee or monthly board meeting. Some can occur at a golf match or other appropriate social events.

It's apparent to me that communication is a key issue here. Would you say the Model's structure contributes to a better flow of information?

Yes, it does. The Corporate Model structure has a built-in communication channel. You don't have just a few people at the top who really know what's going on in a lot of different committees. Instead, you have two major committees—Assessment, Planning and Resource—channeling information to the third major committee—Executive—and then on to the full board. By the time an issue reaches the full board, it has been thoroughly reviewed by many different members. When directors know what's going on, they feel involved with the organization.

You've told us in your e-mails, and you've repeated it again today, that board meetings must be run in an efficient manner. How long do your regular monthly board meetings typically last?

I suspect you've all heard the old proverb that "the number of board members who will attend the next regular meeting depends on how long the last one lasted." As CEO, I keep this in mind. Our regular board meetings usually take seventy-five minutes. Sometimes they run slightly longer.

I might use the term "displaced director" to refer to the board member who can't adapt to the Corporate Model and really wants to be involved with operations. Obviously, some displaced directors resign when the Model is adopted. But some don't. What do you do with them?

You involve them in ways that are perceived as being "hands on." For example, every CEO I know needs help telling the organization's story. If the board member is comfortable doing it, he or she can speak before groups. Another way for him or her to participate is to be one of the directors responsible for the annual assessment of the nonprofit's financial situation.

Or suppose your board is investigating a major new service. Here's an opportunity to put your displaced director on the subcommittee investigating options. The director will be working closely with staff and dealing with an issue that directly impacts the people the organization serves.

Jack, how about some other examples, more routine in nature, showing how directors can be invited to participate in operational areas?

Grant writing. Helping with media relations. Planning annual dinners.

Can you cite some examples showing when the CEO might invite board members to participate in operational decisions?

Here's one from my own experience. My non-profit organization, like so many others in this country, faces severe funding cutbacks. My board decided it was time for our organization to hire a development specialist. Hiring such a person was obviously my responsibility. However, I had had no experience in hiring development specialists. Consequently, I invited two board members who have such experience to advise me in this area. I was still responsible for the person I hired. If the new "hire" was a poor one, I couldn't blame the two board directors.

Everyone needs help to do his or her job from time to time. A CEO has to be mature enough to know his or her own limitations.

If I recall correctly, in one of your letters you said the Corporate Model board should ideally include about eighteen to twenty-four persons. Are all the members of your board truly involved?

I have twenty-five directors on my board. Not everyone is on a standing committee. Some directors are "held in reserve" to tackle special committee projects. These individuals are asked to get involved with one major project each year. The Executive Committee tries to appoint all new directors to a standing committee. This appointment gives them a thorough understanding of how our committee system works.

I'd say when a person first comes on our board he or she may feel uninvolved, but that doesn't last long. Right now, in fact, it seems as if everyone on my board is working on a specific task. It's been a particularly busy year for us.

On the other hand, I don't want to minimize the challenge for both the board chair, and the CEO in keeping board directors involved. As I mentioned in my earlier correspondence with Russ, developing policy isn't inherently as interesting to many people as being involved in the operations of the organization. Consequently, the whole issue of involvement must be a priority issue for both the board chair and the CEO involved.

Russ has just given me a signal that our tee-off time is coming up soon. He's trying to tell me I'd better talk faster if I want to get in nine holes of golf before my plane leaves. So let me just repeat one question that I was asked while getting coffee when I arrived this morning.

One of you asked me what percentage of non-profits actually compensates their board members. The 2010 Board Source study shows that only three percent of boards pay their directors an honorarium. By category, that includes only one percent of charity groups, six percent of trade and professional associations, and 13 percent of foundations. Proponents of compensation maintain that it calls attention to the individual board member's responsibility, even if the compensation amount is nominal.

So, I think we've covered things pretty well this morning. Let me just finish by saying the adoption of the Corporate Model requires the chairperson and the president/CEO to give ongoing attention to maintaining the motivation of board members. Board directors need to know their efforts translate into quality service for clients. Why? Because the board members most likely to feel a commitment are those who take pride in the organization and what it is doing.

Thanks for listening to me last night and again this morning. I hope that these sessions have been helpful.

From: Russ Peterson
Sent: June 14 6:05 PM
To: Jack Billings
Subject: Unanimous recommendation for Model

Jack,

Just want you to know the six of us on the restructuring committee have voted unanimously
to recommend that the Yorkville board adopt the
Corporate Model.

We are comfortable making that recommendation. More important, we're enthusiastic about it.

We are very hopeful that the Yorkville board will
agree with our recommendation. At the very least,
board discussions about the Model will force us
to examine what our nonprofit board does and
how it does it.

It may take some time (probably months) before
the full board makes a decision. When this happens, you will be one of the first to know.

I can't tell you how much I've appreciated your
detailed responses to all of our questions. In particular, thanks for making a personal visit here.
We all gained some very valuable insights. You
state your case very persuasively!

Russ

From: Jack Billings
Sent: June 15 7:58 PM.
To: Russ Peterson
Subject: Great news!

Russ –

I'm pleased about your recommendation! Keep me posted.

I'm particularly glad to have a copy of the transcript, "Board Members Must Be Involved." When I discuss the Corporate Model, I get more questions about this area than any other.

Jack

BTW: What proper engagement by the CEO and involvement by the board all comes down to is simple recognition of the following –

SO MANY DIRECTORS ON NONPROFIT BOARDS ARE BUSY PEOPLE WITH DEMANDING SCHEDULES. THEY NEED TO HAVE CLEAR EVIDENCE THAT THEIR INVOLVEMENT IS MEANINGFUL AND MAKES A REAL DIFFERENCE FOR THE ORGANIZATION AND THE PEOPLE IT SERVES.

From: Russ Peterson
Sent: October 16 8:01 AM.
To: Jack Billings
Subject: Yorkville adopts the Model!

Jack,

Finally, after exhaustive discussion, the Yorkville board has voted to adopt the Corporate Model!

The final vote was taken yesterday. The members of the restructuring group were elated. The final tally was twenty-five directors in favor of the Model, five opposed.

We've got a long road ahead of us, but at least we're *finally* on the right path. We couldn't have done it without you!

Russ

P.S. Will fill you in on more details when I see you at parents' weekend later this month. My son seems to be adjusting to college life!

9

THE CORPORATE MODEL

Two Years Later

From:	Russ Peterson
Sent:	September 30 8:18 PM
To:	Jack Billings
Subject:	Re: Comments on Yorkville's experience
Attachment:	Model plus two years.pdf

Jack,

It's hard to believe it's been nearly two years since we adopted the Model! I'm happy to respond to your recent e-mail asking for comments about Yorkville's experiences with its new governance structure.

And, by the way, before I give you my update, I want to congratulate you on being invited to speak about the Corporate Model at your annual meeting. A national address before one thousand people is pretty impressive. What's more, I think they definitely asked the right person to speak!

I like your idea of surveying other organizations that adopted the Model and summarizing their personal experiences as part of your speech. I'd love to know what you find out, so I can share it with my fellow board members and our CEO. I'm sure the members of the restructuring committee who helped investigate the Model for Yorkville would be especially interested.

Following you'll find my contribution to your speech.

Russ

P.S. Also look for an e-mail I'll forward separately tomorrow. It's an e-mail our new board chair recently sent to the Yorkville staff.

YORKVILLE: THE MODEL
PLUS TWO YEARS

You were right. Change was a challenge. Many of the things you said would happen did, in fact, occur. Among other things, our board chairperson was hard to convince. He completed his term, but asked not to be considered for re-election to the board.

We also lost two long-time board members. One resigned, saying he wished things at Yorkville "could be the way they used to be, when we really felt we were part owners in the place." The other director just said he was "not particularly interested in setting policy." Yet, I'm very happy to report, Yorkville is a much, much stronger organization today than it was when I joined the board.

- Our fiscal problems are under control.
- We've strengthened many programs and eliminated several outmoded ones.
- The board is achieving more, in less time.
- Assessment is much more rigorous. We no longer have the hastily prepared questionnaire or the check-off type of evaluation that used to be typical for our organization.

We've been particularly fortunate to have Joyce Thomas. She has grown professionally in the position and she is an excellent president/CEO. Her sabbatical at a top business program certainly helped her to meet the challenges of moving to the Corporate Model.

We're also been fortunate to have a new board chairperson who is committed to making the Model work. The following story, which happened recently, should give you a good sense of his commitment.

A new board member made an end run to a staff member, saying he really wanted to be involved in programming. The staff member asked the director "to talk to the head of the board." Within twenty-four hours, the board chair called me and asked if I would share a copy of our correspondence, the e-mails that led Yorkville to adopt the

Corporate Model. The board chair said, "Jim's new and so used to doing things the traditional way, I want to give him a full understanding of a volunteer director's role under the Model." I was more than happy to oblige.

In the relatively brief time we've had the Model, I've really come to appreciate the continuing importance of communication at every level in the organization. I know you made it clear to us two years ago that communication really is a key ingredient in the culture change—and IT IS!

Russ

From: Russ Peterson
Sent: October 1 8:22 AM.
To: Jack Billings
Subject: Fwd: Responding to survey results

FYI: see below—this is the e-mail from our new board chair to all staff members

From: A.J. Saunders, Chairman, Yorkville
           Board
Sent: September 6 5:16 PM
To: Yorkville Full Staff
Subject: Responding to survey results

To all staff members,

This summer, the Assessment Committee recommended that our organization communicate more with staff about the vastly different roles of the board and management at Yorkville. The recommendation grew out of discussions held with management following the recent staff survey.

President Joyce Thomas will soon inaugurate a new communication program. This e-mail will give you an overview of the Corporate Model, the innovative board/management structure adopted by Yorkville two years ago.

Under this structure, the board formulates policy and evaluates the organization's operations in carrying out policy. This means that the board's Planning and Resource Committee reviews all proposed programs as to their feasibility. If approved at this level, new programs are sent to the Executive Committee and then to the full board for discussion and final approval.

The ad hoc committees usually develop new policies under which the organization must operate. The Planning and Resource Committee reviews them. The Executive Committee provides the next level of review, after which the policies are sent to the full board with comments for final approval. If policies are approved by the full board, it becomes management's responsibility to see that they are executed properly.

Joyce Thomas is president/CEO and a voting member of the board. She has complete authority over, and responsibility for, all management decisions and functions. She directs the operations of our nonprofit organization in accordance with policy established by the board.

Our structure provides for the annual review of policies and for evaluating achievements against goals.

The board's Assessment Committee is charged with reviewing policies to verify that they are being carried out by management and staff as originally intended. The same committee is also responsible for recommending whether Yorkville should continue, revamp, or discontinue existing programs.

The past two years have been extremely busy for Yorkville. We have clarified responsibilities, started new programs, and discontinued others. We've achieved some major goals and fiscal savings. We have been able to avoid staff layoffs, despite an economy that continues to be difficult.

The board recognizes that its new board/management relationship has led to many changes. Change inevitably created some stress within the organization. The Yorkville board of directors is very much aware of the difficult job the staff has had in these many months of change. We value the spirit of cooperation among staff throughout this period.

Yorkville is moving ahead. In very large measure, our successes are the direct result of the cooperation and dedication you show in meeting your own responsibilities.

Those of us who are on the board are grateful for the support of the staff as we've made the transition! Thank you all!

A.J. Saunders

From: Jack Billings
Sent: October 1 6:48 PM
To: Russ Peterson
Subject: Nice work—CONGRATS

Russ –

Thanks for responding quickly to my request for an update on your experience with the Model. I appreciate it, and I will let you know what feedback I receive!

Your chairperson's e-mail makes it clear that Yorkville knows where it is today and where it's going in the future. I congratulate your board on all that it has achieved.

Jack

BTW: YOUR ORGANIZATION IS NOW IN WORKING ORDER. YOU HAVE SEPARATED POLICY FROM PAPER CLIPS, AND YOU ARE A GROUP READY TO DEAL WITH TWENTY-FIRST-CENTURY DEMANDS!

10

THE MODEL IN ACTION

Real-Life Experiences

From: Jack Billings
Sent: November 15 7:44 PM
To: Russ Peterson
Subject: Speech on the Model
Attachment: CorporateModel.pdf

Russ –

I gave my speech a few days ago, and, though I'm biased, I'd say it went over well. I've had a lot of positive feedback. People were especially interested in the comments of individuals who really live with this Model. Because I drew heavily on our correspondence of two years ago in the early part of the speech, I spoke from notes about how the Model is constructed. I ended the first half of the speech by reading parts of your recent e-mail, with the names deleted.

Attached is an excerpt from the second half of the speech. It's based on actual comments of nonprofit presidents/CEOs who use the Model. My goal in this part of the speech was to give the audience some feel for how other president/CEOs view the Model in practice. It's the only part of the speech I drafted completely. Feel free to share these comments on real life experiences with your colleagues on the board and with Yorkville management.

THE CORPORATE MODEL IN PRACTICE

Whenever I talk about the Corporate Model, I always look for the people in the crowd who are shaking their heads as if to say, "It works for him, but how do we know it works for other people and groups?"

Every large crowd has skeptics, and I can see this audience is no exception. This skepticism might even have increased recently as a result of the trauma caused by Enron, Bernie Madoff, and other organizations and executives.

Having had extensive experience with the Model in a variety of settings—human service agencies, trade associations, national associations, religious groups—I have yet to find a single organization that reversed course and returned to the traditional community model structure. However, a few have gone to the extreme of eliminating all committees, and some have over-delegated to the extent the board meets only two or three times a year.

But I did some extra homework and came prepared to answer questions, since I'm assuming by your presence here that you are curious how the Model works in practice.

Up to this point, I've talked primarily about the role of the board under the Model, using a number of telling comments from my friend Russ. So now, it's management's turn at the podium.

William Bowen, the president emeritus of the Andrew W. Mellon Foundation and former Princeton University president, once said that "finding the appropriate balance between executive authority and board oversight is more likely to require strengthening the hand of the CEO than building up the powers of the board."

When I was asked to speak, I knew I wanted to describe in a very tangible way what the impact of strengthening the CEO's hand means to an organization. At the same time, I wanted you to get the sense that the Model does not just come in plain vanilla—but in a rainbow of flavors.

So about six weeks ago, I sat down and made a list of not-for-profit groups operating under the Model. I pared my list to eleven organizations that vary in terms of size, budget, and the length of time they've operated under the Model. Most of them have about one hundred employees, although they range from a low of seventy staff members to a high of two thousand employees. Their annual budgets range from $3.5 million to $60 million, with a number of organizations clustered around the $6 million mark. (Note: that's in 2010 dollars.) Their time with the Model is as brief as two years and as long as ten years.

After making my list, I called the eleven president/CEOs heading these organizations. I asked about ten questions, from "How well has the Model served your organization?" to "What are the financial benefits?" But these questions were just to frame the interview. What I was really looking for was their take on their own experience.

Every one of them reported being happy with the Model, but two said they would be happier if their nonprofits had made them voting members of the board. One commented, however, that not being a board member made it possible for her to advocate for her organization's mission and not be constrained by fiscal concerns.

Although this may seem like an unusual viewpoint, this CEO finds some value in acting essentially as an outside consultant would act. I know from her later comments that on a day-to-day basis, she is not actually free from fiscal constraints. Like the others I interviewed, she's counting dollars carefully these days.

Every organization I interviewed had reduced its committee structure. One had gone so far as to have only two standing committees, while another had cut back to EIGHT. Virtually everyone, it seemed, was happiest about getting rid of standing board personnel committees.

What impressed me most, however, was how consistently they felt the board structure had empowered them and their organizations. Here are some of their comments:

It assisted us in the rapid development of a work plan. The Model appeals to "fast track" board people who want to get things done.

It has freed me to take our mission and policies and implement them in an efficient way.

With the Model, we have the ability to be more competitive in a rapidly changing environment.

As president, I have clout when dealing with others. The title gives me entree to and equity with business executives.

And finally, a very poignant comment from a CEO who finds that the Corporate Model provides a very different work environment from what he'd known in the traditional nonprofit world.

The Model gets away from the "do what we (the board) want you to do" syndrome. (As you know, this can be a debilitating feature of the traditional model.)

Another impression gained from these interviews was how clearly everyone understood their roles. Repeatedly, the top executive mentioned that the line between staff and board members was no longer fuzzy. The Model had clearly defined CEO, board director, and staff roles. In the words of one top exec, "the Model defines the roles of the players extremely well and determines what is appropriate or not."

Staff members, one manager noted, also feel like empowered professionals. The overall message was that management in these organizations is spending more time doing things that need to be done rather than spending a daunting amount of time responding to board requests for assistance in making operating decisions.

While doing these interviews—they took about thirty to forty-five minutes for each one—I refrained from making comments of my own about the Model. I wanted their words, not mine.

When I asked, "What are the differences between the Corporate Model and the traditional or community model? These are the responses I received:

It's more efficient, there is so much to be done. It conserves time resources. The community model encumbered management. This makes wise use of volunteer time.

I wouldn't work under the community model. The emotional connection often fostered under the community model is not necessarily good.

People in the business world really understand how it works. That's a built-in advantage.

It requires the president to be more of a risk taker.

There's more emphasis on strategy.

All of this sounds pretty good. But obviously, any governance structure that is this different has disadvantages as well as advantages. Or if you're an optimist, as I am, you'll consider them problems to overcome.

Maintaining connection with board members is simply easier to do, one respondent said, with the "feel good" approach of the community model. There's also an adjustment period for board members who have "extra" time on their hands and who want to be operationally involved, some noted.

A colleague of mine once observed that directors who have too much time to contribute can be just as problematic as directors who don't have enough time. I'm sure many of you can relate to either of these scenarios. The other two major disadvantages I heard about in my interviews can be summarized in these two statements:

Fund-raising can be more difficult because there's less (board) involvement.

The Corporate Model is too cognitive in character...the heart is missing.

At the same time, the executives often countered these statements, with action-oriented language of their own. Statements like, "When it comes to fund-raising, the president just needs to motivate board members to do the job."

Or this statement, which actually parallels my own view:

Finding responsible and useful tasks for people who take board positions to feel good about what they are doing will always be a challenge.

Many of the people I interviewed were pleased with the way the Corporate Model has helped their organizations grow. Several noted their not-for-profit groups had tripled or quadrupled in size over the course of a few years. These same execs said their organizations were not growing under the community model. But growth within the organization actually was defined in different ways by different top execs. For example, one said:

Our organization is clearly more entrepreneurial. This opens doors in the business world. Business titles enable you to approach business-people or donors without feeling you're going "hat-in-hand."

Others pointed out the Model helped them attract very talented people to the nonprofit sector. Many of these same recruits, they told me, were turned off by the traditional model and its slow decision-making processes.

And, finally, one said his organization just gets more respect: *The United Way and others respect a policymaking board when they review one.*

I also asked my interviewees if they could list some financial benefits of the Corporate Model. They noted the routine savings, like not having to buy as many lunches for board members or not spending "$1,000 in process costs to save $100."

They also spoke of financial benefits that were more dramatic. One not-for-profit president/CEO said that his nonprofit had been dependent on the United Way for 70 percent of its funds before adopting the Corporate Model but now needed only 30 percent of its funds from this charitable organization.

Another CEO said her nonprofit, which is a sheltered workshop, is now well positioned to sell services to business organizations. Others reported savings related to staff administrative time, which they estimated at about three to four days per month.

My final questions were about the effectiveness of the assessment process, and the time it took their organizations to move to the Corporate Model. In both cases, the responses varied significantly.

One group does not have either an assessment process or an assessment committee. It depends on the United Way as well as state and national accrediting processes to evaluate the organization. Others have very rigorous processes to evaluate both internal and external environments. Many look to progress in their strategic plans to set the benchmarks for evaluations.

Overall, these eleven nonprofits moved to the Corporate Model in as short a period as one year or as long as five years. The way it happened in all cases can be summed up in a single phrase:

STRONG LEADERSHIP MADE IT HAPPEN!

11

THE MODEL VS. TRADITION

An Overview of the Differences

From: Jack Billings
Sent: November 17 7:14 AM.
To: Russ Peterson
Subject: Nearly forty differences in models

Russ –

When I sent the excerpt from my speech high-lighting the comments of president/CEOs in the real world, I forgot to include something I think you'll find interesting.

I put together a handout for distribution at the national meeting. It simply lists the important differences—nearly forty of them—between the Corporate Model and the traditional nonprofit model.

Thought you'd appreciate seeing it.

CORPORATE MODEL VS. TRADITIONAL MODEL WHAT'S DIFFERENT?

CORPORATE	TRADITIONAL
Represents New Approach To Board Governance	Has Strength Via Years of Tradition
Simplifies Board Organization Structure	Creates Complex Board Organization Structure
Utilizes Board Talents for Policy Issues	Has Board Addressing Policy & Operations
Does Not Involve Board In Operations	Takes Staff Time to Orient, Educate Board
Makes Use of Staff Input For Key Decisions	Places Lower Value on Staff Input
Allows for Fewer Board Members	Allows for Greater Number of Board Members
Keeps Communication Lines Clear	Tends to Create Complex Lines of Communication
Includes Fewer Topics on Board Agendas	Often Includes Minor Operating Items on Agenda
Reduces Time Needed to Make Decisions	Have to Increase Time to Make Decisions
Board Only Hires CEO	Hires CEO, Other Personnel
Board Assess CEO & Organization Rigorously	Board Assesses Management More Informally

Board Involvement and Communication

CORPORATE	TRADITIONAL
Formally Structures Organization	Develops Less Formal Organization
Pinpoints & Clarifies Responsibility	Promotes Shared Responsibility & Blame
Builds Staff Professionalism	Board Can Direct Staff – Staff Can Be "Servants"
Allows More Management Flexibility	Staff Often Must Wait Too Long For Board Decisions
Allows More Management. Risk Taking	Board & Executive Director Share Risk Taking
Full-time President/CEO	Volunteer Part-time President/CEO
Orients CEO to Strong Management Style	Board. Involvement Allows for Weaker Top Executive
More Ad Hoc - Fewer Standing Committees	Many Standing Committees
Less Staff Time to Support Board Committees	More Staff Time Supporting Board Committees
Focus on Productivity	More Focus on "Feelings"
Board Structure Supports Growth Periods	Operating Difficulties During Growth Periods – Slow to Take Advantage of Opportunities

CORPORATE	TRADITIONAL
Creates Bottoms Up Budget Process	Creates Top Down Budget Process
Establishes Checks & Balances System	Allows Informal Checks & Balances
Except for Budget, Board Not Involved in Fiscal Processes	Board Heavily Involved (e.g., check signing, routine contracts)
Cost Effective	Not Cost Effective

Management of the Organization -- Financial Operations

CORPORATE	TRADITIONAL
Trust is Critical in Culture	Board & Exec Can Have "Parent-Child" Relationship
President/CEO Is Often Voting Board Member	Executive Director Is Not Board Member
More Effort to Get Board Involvement	Board Is Involved in Operations
CEO Is Spokesperson	Volunteer President Is Spokesperson
Corporate Titles Understood by Public	Executive Director Title Has Wide Ranging Operational Meaning
President/CEO Can Overstep Authority	Traditions Limit Executive Director Authority
Staff "End Runs" to Board Unacceptable	Staff "End Runs" to Board Tolerated
Challenge to Motivate Board Members	Board Members Are Involved in Operational Details

CORPORATE	TRADITIONAL
Clear Separation of Policy & Operations	Tradition Defines Management – Results in Volunteer Assistance in Operations
Planning Issues Have Priority	Allows Planning to be Postponed
Major Focus on Clients/Members	Major Focus on Processes

Interpersonal Relations -- Policy Development

12

IS YOUR ORGANIZATION READY
FOR THE CORPORATE MODEL?

*The Model Is About
Structure and People*

The following questions and answers can further help you assess whether the Corporate Model is right for your organization. In attempting to apply this information, you should take into account the personalities, the culture, and the management situation in your own organization. The Corporate Model is not only about structure but also about people, which is why no book about the Corporate Model can ever be truly complete. Each nonprofit organization that adopts the Model must write its own ending.

Q. *What kinds of nonprofit boards are most likely to be attracted to the Corporate Model?*

A. Nonprofit boards experiencing some internal dissension and boards that are constantly bogged down in detail. Also, the Corporate Model will appeal to many nonprofit boards that are operating satisfactorily but wish to become more efficient and effective. Members of these boards realize that with the Corporate Model, they could be even more productive. After adopting the Model, some boards also find there's revived interest by board members who were thinking of resigning early. I can't tell you how many times I have heard busy professionals say that they simply will not serve on any nonprofit boards because of slow decision making about operational details.

Q. *I thought there was only one Corporate Model. Can it be utilized in different ways?*

A. The Corporate Model has one general framework. Its major feature is the separation of policy and operations. How this separation is accomplished can vary from organization to organization. In addition, four other characteristics clearly distinguish the Corporate Model from more traditional board structures. These are fewer committees, fewer board meetings, fewer "surprises," and greater top-management accountability.

Q. *Very often the people who serve on for-profit boards are the same people who serve on non-profit boards. Given this scenario, why have so many volunteer directors tended, over time, to function less efficiently on nonprofit boards than on for-profit boards?*

A. It has a great deal to do with tradition and the level of financial risk involved. In for-profit groups, directors may well have a personal, financial stake in the success of the organization. They can be financially at risk if the organization is operated inefficiently or ineffectively. Generally, unless they make very negligent decisions, nonprofit boards are not at risk financially. (Caution: don't underestimate the modest risks involved. These can be related to whether the volunteer is president/CEO; the organization runs afoul of the Intermediate Sanctions Acts; or there is gross negligence involved, such as not monitoring governmental payments of withholding on income taxes.)

Q. *Nonprofit X has a board in name only. Board members are prominent individuals, but not very active. The organization now finds it needs more involvement from its board. Will the Corporate Model work for this organization?*

A. Yes. Discuss the Corporate Model with all board members. Talk about the various responsibilities directors have and, in particular, the board's policy-making function. Explain that the Model enables the president/CEO to request board members' time only for the development and assessment of policy issues. The key points to stress are that their time commitments will not be extensive and wise use will be made of the time they give to the organization. In fact, wise use of volunteer time is one of the most appealing inducements for joining a Corporate Model board.

Q. *How long does it take to be completely comfortable with the Corporate Model?*

A. It takes at least several years of operation. It may take some boards even longer—to the point where all directors have come on the board under the Corporate Model structure.

Q. *What types of board members are most likely to oppose the adoption of the Corporate Model?*

A. Some process-oriented directors (individuals who are never quite done examining things from all angles) tend to hold back their full approval for the Corporate Model. Though they don't view it this way, they tend to like the hands-on involvement that comes from the parent-child board structure. Some directors may be hostile to the concept because they do not want to give up power. Some of these individuals may not exercise managerial direction in their own jobs. Others are not satisfied with their jobs and seek satisfaction through their work on a nonprofit board. They may not want to give up the influence they can exercise over operations in the nonprofit organization.

Q. *What types of board members do you want on the Corporate Model board?*

A. The Corporate Model does not exclude any particular personality or occupational background. Board directors who have operated well under the Model include full-time homemakers, ministers, labor leaders, business executives, human service personnel, physicians, community volunteers, and others. The common denominator that makes individuals effective as board directors is their interest in the organization's mission and establishing and monitoring policy that supports it. Conversely, these same individuals often have a low tolerance for being involved with operational details (e.g., routine office maintenance, basic IT purchases needed for operations). Usually they understand the importance of addressing issues in terms of concept and /or strategy. Most important, these individuals can work within a policy environment without becoming bored. They like having a good handle on the organization's direction. They have little need for the continual interpersonal operational interaction and immediate operational gratification that characterize the culture of the traditional nonprofit board. The truly outstanding Corporate Model board directors have excellent vision.

While a traditional board needs a broad range of talents and skills to address operational needs, it is not quite the same for boards operating under the Model. Although you want diversity, in terms of individual backgrounds and development skills and contacts, you need to keep one requirement in focus when recruiting new directors. You need individuals with vision.

Q. *What do you do about a truly hostile board member—one staunchly opposed to the Model even though it has been adopted?*

A. Whatever the reason for the hostility, it is difficult to have such a personality on your board. Sometimes other directors these individuals respect can convince them that the organization is better served by the Model. Sometimes diplomacy, particularly on the part of the board chairperson, is sufficient. Other times you can only wait until their terms expire or they decide to leave the board.

Q. *How long does it take to institute the Corporate Model?*

A. It generally takes about a year from the time the board adopts it. Change never occurs steadily or smoothly. There are always highs and lows in the process. Remember, it takes education and constant repetition to make the Model more than a structural outline. It also takes leadership and persuasion to make the Model work. The role of the board chairperson in this process is critical. Also remember that the Model needs to be reassessed about every five years. If new board members do not fully understand the Model, the board may tend to fall back into traditional ways of operating, and a new board training program may be required.

Q. *What does the meeting agenda typically include for a board operating under the Corporate Model?*

A. When setting the agenda, remember that you have two chief objectives: to stay focused on policy issues and to conserve board members' time. Use the following outline when you determine the flow of your board meetings.

Meeting Flow
- Review of last meeting minutes
- Review of financial statements
- Old business
- New business
- Report by president on operations
- Reports by other managers (e.g., medical director)
- Board information and education

Q. *How often should a Corporate Model board meet?*

A. In general, Corporate Model boards meet less often than do boards structured under the traditional model. Not-for-profit groups operating in a local area tend to find six to eight meetings a year sufficient. Some organizations have gone to quarterly meetings, but often, this level of contact is insufficient to build a cohesive team spirit among volunteer directors. Some national groups meet only two times a year. However, many other national groups have found they need to hold board meetings more often than every six months.

Conference calls are a good way to hold additional meetings, even if they are legally required meetings allowed by state laws. Electronic software systems are now available for efficiently scheduling these calls. Given Internet options today, conference calling can be inexpensive. Also, because of time-compressed lifestyles and travel expenses, some regional and national nonprofit organizations often hold meetings via conference call or electronic media.

Regardless of how many meetings the full board has, the Model requires more meetings for ad hoc committees and the Executive Committee. These are key meetings, during which the most basic work takes place.

Q. *Do Corporate Model boards set a dollar limit on the president/CEO's fiscal discretion?*

A. The president/CEO has complete discretion as long as he or she works within the budget and budgetary guidelines. However, if any major changes are needed, the board must approve them. For example, if the president/CEO finds resources budgeted for capital improvements are not needed, he or she cannot simply move these funds to the salary account without board approval. Most organizations need to borrow money on a short-term basis to meet cash-flow requirements. The CEO needs to have complete discretion to act in such situations. Consequently, the board needs to pass a formal resolution authorizing a fiscal limit for borrowing. In practice, this limit is typically dependent upon the needs of the organization and the level of confidence the board has in the CEO.

Q. *How is the president/CEO's job description developed?*

A. By the Executive Committee or an ad hoc committee, with final approval by the full board. It must reflect the needs of the nonprofit organization and the board should periodically review it. The CEO can also request a change. Such requests are usually related to growth in the organization.

Q. *How does a president/CEO turn down advice about operations from the board?*

A. With difficulty. It all depends on the kind of culture that has been established on the board. Ideally, the president/CEO should be comfortable saying, "Thank you for your suggestions. I have considered them, but I feel these matters should be handled differently." For example, on one board on which I served, the board wanted the president/CEO to employ a COO because the CEO traveled a great deal, and many board members felt he needed more internal help. The CEO was an excellent entrepreneurial type who conscientiously felt that budget constraints precluded employing a COO. It took about four years of negotiation to motivate him to make the change, which turned out to be a highly successful one. In this case, a culture of mutual trust was present so that the board accepted his rationale for not hiring a COO for such a long period.

Q. *Under the Corporate Model, how should the board respond if the president/CEO makes a mistake?*

A. No one does a job perfectly. If this mistake is one in a series of serious errors, the president / CEO might need to be replaced. Directors should consider the CEO's total record and carefully weigh the seriousness of the mistake.

Q. *Is the Corporate Model situational? Would it work fine for President A, but have to be modified considerably for President B?*

A. No. The Corporate Model is adopted for the organization, not the individual. When a not-for-profit organization chooses a new president, it requires that the responsibilities of the new president/CEO be the same as those of the old one, except for financial background or experience with nonprofit organizations. Then stronger financial, general administrative or volunteer backup is needed. A crucial requirement for the Corporate Model board is to find the right person to do the job.

Q. *What happens when a nonprofit organization changes presidents?*

A. The board must find a new president who understands the Corporate Model and feels secure with it. I have found that it has been a great recruitment tool. The individual must be a strong person. Immediately, he or she will be faced with a whole set of responsibilities not generally found in a more traditional structure. The person must want to assume—and has to be able to assume—this level of responsibility.

Q. *How does the Corporate Model board know when to discharge a president/CEO?*

A. When the president is not meeting agreed goals and objectives or is meeting them in illegal, immoral, or inept ways. Leadership is critical. You'll know if it's missing.

Q. *Does the Corporate Model board ever take over for an inept president?*

A. The board may have to become involved if it dismisses a president. The arrangement is temporary and continues only until a replacement can be hired. Otherwise, the board has no excuse for becoming involved in management. If the board has to manage for the president, then that president shouldn't be there.

Q. *How are reasonable disagreements over whether an issue is a policy or operational question resolved?*

A. The board makes the final decision on where to draw the line. In a case of opposing views, it's up to the president/CEO to make the most persuasive argument for his or her position. Though the board and president/CEO are partners, the board is the ultimate authority.

Q. *How do you persuade an unusually influential board member to reduce his or her interest in operational issues?*

A. Every board has this problem. The Corporate Model board is no exception. Every situation is handled according to the personality involved. Proceed with great care.

Q. *How is board succession handled under the Model?*

A. In very much the same manner as under the traditional model. Typically, directors are elected initially for two- or three-year terms, and they can be re-elected for one or two additional terms. In some nonprofits, directors can serve again after a year's absence from the board. This procedure is not recommended for the Corporate Model board because the Model depends on a flow of new ideas and viewpoints.

Boards need to be aware of the need to keep the Model's structure intact. As new directors with traditional board experience come aboard, there may be a tendency to add more board standing committees. Adding more and more committees will eventually undermine the structure—and defeat the purpose of the Model. As a result, the structure can return to a traditional one without anyone ever casting a vote for the change.

Because the CEO is likely to be the person who is the one "constant" throughout turnover of volunteers and staff, he or she is responsible for working with the board chair to train and educate new directors in the processes and values of the Corporate Model. This ongoing educational process must continue for years because the Model is still considered a new and, to some people, radical structure of governance.

Q. *When can board members get involved in operational areas?*

A. Only when they are invited to do so by the president/CEO. At these times, let me stress again, they are not acting as board members.

Q. *Can a board member ever wear another "hat" in an organization?*

A. Sometimes a board member acts not as a director but as a different kind of volunteer. For example, Director Z has a particular accounting skill and wants to utilize it to help the nonprofit. The CEO agrees. In this instance, the board member is not a board member, but a volunteer working under the direction of the CEO. This distinction is easy to understand if you think about the example of a Boy Scout leader who serves as a troop's scoutmaster and serves as a board member on a Boy Scout regional council. As scoutmaster, he follows scouting guidelines and directives from the professionals. As a council director, he helps set policy for the Scout movement in that geographic area. In both instances, he is a volunteer. In only one instance does he act as a director.

Q. *Nonprofit boards have many challenges, such as inadequate time on their agendas for strategic planning, overcommitted chairs, poor evaluation processes for their top executives, poor committee outcomes, crises, and transition problems. Could Lead Directors help improve nonprofit board performance?*

A. Publically traded corporations are required to have one independent board member named Lead Director when the board chair also holds the CEO title. This is required by the New York Stock Exchange, starting about 2002, for listed companies as one way to ensure independent director control of the board. (Independent control is not an issue with nonprofits.) A first generation of Lead Directors is addressing problems similar to the nonprofit ones cited in your question. Through focusing on these problems, Lead

Directors report they are strengthening board/ CEO relationships. To date, I have not heard of any nonprofit organization experimenting with a version of the Lead Director. However, I won't be surprised if that happens. If it does, just as in the for-profit world, the person holding the position would have to be a catalyst in terms of process and be careful not to cause conflict between the nonprofit CEO and the volunteer board chair. Obviously, he or she has to be well respected by the entire board.

According to the 2010 Board Source survey, the following areas are the ones that chief executives and board directors cite as needing most improvement:

- Fund-raising
- Strategic planning
- Focus (more strategic, less operational)
- Board composition and diversity
- Board member commitment, engagement, attendance
- Board self-assessment
- Board recruitment
- Board development/orientation

Based on these research results, it would seem that the CEOs of many boards could use a Lead Director to garner better outcomes in the above areas.

Q. *What if the staff complains that the organization has become "too formal" under the Corporate Model?*

A. The Model is a formal structure but it is also a human one. Any organization that grows and becomes more complex needs a more formal structure and a clearly defined communication channel. The Model provides both. Communication is critically important. The president/CEO, in particular must be very aware of the need to communicate effectively with all parts of the organization. The Corporate Model sounds businesslike, but it is not cold and uncaring.

Q. *Doesn't the Corporate Model mimic what takes place in the profit sector?*

A. To some extent, yes, but with one key difference. The Corporate Model board in the nonprofit arena must conduct a finer performance audit than most business organizations conduct. That's because there is no fiscal bottom line on which to judge performance, except that expenses must match income. In addition, so much of what a nonprofit does must ultimately be measured with imperfect metrics. (See next Q&A.)

Q. *If a traditionally structured not-for-profit group isn't ready to adopt the full Corporate*

Model, can it compromise and adopt parts of the Model?

A. Boards in this situation can take three steps and still benefit significantly.

First, within the current structure, try to give more responsibilities to the executive director. Examine all powers and responsibilities now held by the board and determine where shifts can be made. Ask questions: Does the board really need a physical facilities committee? Can responsibility for physical facilities be delegated to management with intermittent oversight by the board?

The next step is to review the board's entire committee structure. Are all the committees the board currently has necessary? How many committees are wasting valuable volunteer time? All too frequently, committees are established simply because managers want "to keep volunteers involved." If you examine the activities of these committees, you'll find they generally amount to nothing more than busy work. Make sure every board committee, over time, is making wise use of volunteer time.

The third and most important step is to ensure that the board rigorously evaluates the top executive and the organization. The volunteer president (or board chair) should not be doing it alone. A committee that assesses and analyzes every important aspect of the organization in some depth should do the evaluation. In many nonprofits, some important evaluation measures must be *imperfect.* The cost of developing measures that are more precise is prohibitive. Consequently, the committee and CEO must deal with metrics that are anecdotal, subjective, interpretive, or qualitative. Likely, the metrics will rely on a small sample, uncontrolled situational factors, or cannot be precisely replicated. Where these types of measures are employed, both the committee and the operating manager need to agree on the processes and that the outcomes constitute fair and reasonably trustworthy information. However, the overall objective of the committee should be to assess policy outcomes, not count paper clips, and to allow time for the board to spend time on generative planning. Directors' questions in the generative mode are different than the questions they ask when day-to-day operations take up the agenda because directors will find themselves focused on identifying available opportunities and vulnerabilities. Both management and the board need to be on the same page.

Q. *Across the U.S., nonprofits have been slow to adopt the Corporate Model. Why?*

A. There are many reasons, including tradition, executive director reluctance, rhetoric, and human inertia. When it comes to making a cultural change, tradition is a powerful master. Individuals who have been involved with the traditional model understand it and are comfortable with the way it operates. Despite its many limitations, it is still a known quantity. In addition, involvement with the details of the organization's activities is often very interesting and appealing to many volunteers. That makes it easy for volunteer directors to overlook the fact that the board structure is less results oriented than it could be.

Another reason for the slow growth of the Corporate Model is the reluctance of executive directors to assume more responsibility. It is not unusual for an executive director in a traditionally structured nonprofit to be shocked at the level of responsibility the executive head of the Corporate Model organization must shoulder. Many executive directors are comfortable presenting alternatives to the board, and then withdrawing from the decision-making process. This is a "safe" way to operate. If the board makes a poor decision, the executive director can't be blamed. On the other hand, if the decision is on target, it's easy for the executive director to claim credit because he or she recommended it in the first place. Rhetoric is another factor. This simply means that when the benefits of the Corporate Model are discussed, too many people talk it to death by calling for "volunteer involvement" and "organization ownership." The final factor is human inertia—probably the biggest barrier for the Corporate Model. Change is difficult and stressful; many directors simply don't want to address the need for change on their boards.

Q. *Why is the Corporate Model sometimes called the "Model of Accountability"?*

A. On more traditional boards, where directors participate in operational decisions, it is difficult to determine responsibility. The Corporate Model pinpoints accountability much better than any other nonprofit board structure. When it is properly utilized, there is little equivocation as to who is responsible.

Q. *What is the single most important advantage· of the Corporate Model?*

A. It motivates your nonprofit to look ahead to the future.

Q. *What else can you tell us about the role of nonprofit boards as they have evolved in the twenty-first century?*

A. Attorney Barbara Blackford, when writing in *The Conference Board Review,* put it well, and below I summarize her key messages. Blackford maintains that directors should have objectivity that staff intimately involved with operations may lack. She has proposed and—as an advocate for a strategically focused nonprofit board model providing generative input—we strongly agree with her that boards should:

- Convey respect of management's knowledge, expertise, and experience without rubber-stamping management decisions.
- Be ever mindful of the board's strategic role, in contrast to substituting preferences for day-to-day matters that do not affect strategy.
- Prepare well for board and committee meetings.
- When possible and appropriate, the board should provide an opportunity for management to understand potential questions or issues in advance of meetings so that all directors have access to meaningful information.
- Every director should always ask the question on his or her mind and press for an answer—at the appropriate time.

In response, management should:

- Respect the board's role, including its role in setting corporate strategy and overseeing the organization's operational performance against that strategy.
- Facilitate the board's strategic focus by spending the time needed to provide the right information to the board in a digestible and understandable format. (Blackford maintains that a board engulfed with unneeded detail will struggle to be effective or strategic.)
- Understand that directors have the right to full, fair, and complete answers to their questions.
- Provide the resources needed for directors to fulfill their role effectively.

In addition to what Bickford has outlined, as a matter of basic principle, a board should:

- Understand and be able to publically articulate its mission.
- Be engaged, informed, and independent.
- Be alert to conflicts of interest and potential fraud.

"Since our switch to the Model we've served more people at less time and cost."